Real Life

Also by Michael Lesy

Wisconsin Death Trip

Real Life

Louisville in the Twenties

by Michael Lesy

PANTHEON BOOKS, NEW YORK

To Liz and Nadia

Copyright © 1976 by Michael Lesy

All the photographs in this book are from the Caufield and Shook Collection of the Photographic Archives of the University of Louisville, with the exception of the photographs on pages 19, 113, 181, 235, and 237, which are from the Potter Collection, and the aerial photograph on page 5, by Park Aerial Surveys, Inc., Louisville, Kentucky.

The stories in this book attributed to criminal or civil court cases or to clinical records are based upon actual events but fictitious names have been substituted for the real names of the persons who were involved.

Library of Congress Cataloging in Publication Data

Lesy, Michael, 1945 –
Real Life: Louisville in the Twenties.

Includes bibliographical references.
    1.   Louisville, Ky. – Social conditions.   I.   Title.
HN80.L78L48   309.1′769′44   76-9977
ISBN 0-394-49813-5
ISBN 0-394-73235-9 pbk.

Designed by Stevan A. Baron

Manufactured in the United States of America

First Edition

Table of Contents

Acknowledgments

My respects to Walker Evans, who was infatuated with ordinary things; my special thanks to Warren Susman for his books and ideas; to David Logan for his suggestions; to Grady Clay for his care and criticism; to Bryan Wilkins for his hospitality, affection, and advice; to Bruce and Patty Mann for their affection and advice; and to Ted and Bridgette Wathen for their affection.

My thanks to John C. Anderson, Director of the Photographic Archives, University of Louisville, for his generous help; to Ken Strothman for printing the pictures, and to Barbara Crawford for her help; to Mark Harris, head of the Kentucky Division, Louisville Free Public Library, for his help and friendship, and to assistant librarians Darlene Roby and Marion Turner for their help; to Edward Davis for his interviews of retired black working men, to Richard Sheridan for his friendship, his research assistance, and his interviews of retired white working men, and to Charles Coddington for his help; to Louis Bellardo, Assistant Director, Kentucky State Archives and Records, for doing everything he could; and to Robert DeBurger, Director of Research and Special Projects, Kentucky Department for Human Resources, for his authorization.

I am grateful to the American Council of Learned Societies, with whose generous support this book was written.

Introduction

This book is about people who passed through the First War on their way to the Great Depression. During the war, they had experienced government intervention and regulation of their food, their labor, and their thoughts more severe than their grandparents had experienced during the Civil War. The ones who could least afford it had been rewarded with an inflationary increase in the wholesale price index of 108 points between 1914 and 1918.[1] Even those who had profited from the war were crushed by the severe depression of 1921, when the same wholesale price index fell 79 points.[2] The good times of 1923–1928 seemed even better to people who had survived such confusion.

This book is composed of artifacts made by men who pretended to record the truth and transmit information. The most convincing of these pretensions are the legal depositions from the Jefferson County civil and criminal courts, and the medical transcripts from the Central State Mental Hospital of Kentucky. The least convincing are the photographs made by the Louisville firm of Caufield and Shook, and the newspaper accounts derived or excerpted from the Louisville *Herald, Herald Post, Louisville Post, Evening Post,* Louisville *Times,* and Louisville *Courier-Journal.* The newspaper accounts, the photographs, the medical transcripts, and the legal depositions are all middle-class re-creations and transpositions. They are extended analogies in which the world is made into something already recognizable. They are not real. They are forms of art and literature. The written documents have been supplemented with health, employment, and income statistics and with random interviews of old men with good memories.

The photographs have been arranged so as to resemble sequences edited from a film. The items of the text have been so placed, one with the other, as to resemble a crossword puzzle freed of its frame. The text is intended to elaborate not illustrate the photographs.

The archival collection of photographs originally made by the firm of Caufield and Shook are tableaus of commercial surreality. They provide evidence of a city culture whose willful manipulation of facts, confusion of people with objects, and minute-by-minute recording of fabricated events differs greatly from the matter-of-fact, human-centered, seasonally paced farm town culture that had preceded it. Caufield and Shook had half a dozen competitors, but few could rival the firm's ability to give their customers what they wanted. The firm's pictures are sometimes so retouched that the people in them look like stage props. Their customers thought nothing of asking them to take twenty pictures of the inside of a battery factory filled with fumes, rot, and congealed lead, and then expecting them to retouch the pictures so that the fumes became sunlight pouring through walls that had been turned into windows. Caufield and Shook made photographs of automobile wrecks for insurance companies and of bedsprings for mattress companies in the same spirit that small town photographers in the nineteenth-century made portraits of young couples and whole families. The firm photographed women who were romantically involved with vacuum cleaners, and men who quietly talked with refrigerators. They used the attentive presence of black servants and the grins of pretty white girls as motifs in imaginary tableaus where stunning happi-

vii

ness was associated with soft drinks and telephones. A generation before, people had had their photographs made to mark such real occasions as a birth, a marriage, or a death. In Louisville in 1924, Caufield and Shook obliged one client with a dozen pictures, from six different angles, on two separate backgrounds, of a chocolate chip cookie. Most of the people they photographed wore costumes or disguises. They made hundreds of pictures of crowds of men wearing capes, fezes, gowns, satin vests, leather aprons, jeweled belts, false beards, and fake eyelashes. They photographed dozens of garden parties attended by princes and fairies. The firm served the commercial middle class who recorded their private lives with snapshots, but wore masks in public. They satisfied their customers by taking photographs the way forgers made documents.

When members of the middle class were overwhelmed by their own appetites and lost hold of their masks in public, they appeared on the front pages of the newspapers. Reporters pretended to be police detectives looking for clues, but they behaved like entertainers looking for droll misfortunes. Stories of lust and stories of greed were the most popular. Homicides and embezzlements became biographical melodramas: a certain kind of character became a predictable kind of fate. The news read as if it had been written by a staff of burlesque comedians who had once been Baptist ministers. Within its literary pattern, members of the middle class became boors, charlatans, cuckolds, and run-arounds. Members of the working class appeared as alcoholics, pathetically inept criminals, or victims of industrial accidents. Blacks became ironic jokes,

drug dealers, and thieves. The only respectable people were the very rich men who owned the newspapers, held public office, and occasionally argued with one another.

The records of the state mental hospital and county courts contain evidence of human choices so disastrous but so ordinary that the newspapers could use them only occasionally. The papers rarely printed stories of lunatics, and merely listed divorces, two or three times a week, like baseball scores. Very few members of the white middle class and very few blacks appear in the divorce depositions. There are reasons: Most middle-class couples who decided to get divorced kept quiet in public and paid their lawyers to file whatever formulaic expressions of discontent were necessary to divide their lives and their property. Few blacks owned enough to make such divorce proceedings necessary, or to pay for them. However, members of the white working class had just enough property to lose and just enough propriety to argue about. The divorce court records are filled with their bitter accusations and purloined love letters.[3] For somewhat different reasons, their sufferings also dominate the medical transcripts from the state mental hospital. Members of the white middle class were able to avoid this hospital because they either could afford private care, or could sufficiently disguise and indulge their preoccupations and addictions. Blacks were rarely transcribed although often committed because the white medical secretaries and psychiatrists were either uninterested in them or could not understand them. Once again, the white working class had just enough sanity to lose, and just enough in common with their doctors to be understood. In spite of this, the medical secretaries often failed to record their ecstatic syntax. Whites also appear with more frequency than blacks in the criminal depositions, if not in the police statistics, of the decade. Once whites were arrested, they were more inclined than blacks to argue with the police, and the police went to more trouble to collect evidence to make cases against them. In contrast, blacks were arrested, charged, and almost always sentenced without litigation. In either case, police stenographers took depositions that were often incomplete and made transcripts that were barely literate. These broken depositions, piecemeal transcripts, and incomplete medical records are all that remain of the ordinary people who leapt into the arms of the state like suicides from a burning building. The middle classes left no such traces. Instead they left headlines full of disasters and retouched photographs cluttered with objects. These art forms, illusions, sufferings, and visions are the primary historical documents of the decade.

Notes

1. U.S. Department of Labor, *Statistical Abstracts of the U.S.*, 1924–1928 (Washington, D.C.: U.S. Government Printing Office).
2. *Ibid.*
3. The records appear to duplicate evidence of sadism, impotence, and frigidity collected by Wilhelm Reich in his psychoanalytic clinic in Vienna in 1922, and alluded to by Robert and Helen Lynd in *Middletown* (New York: Harcourt, Brace & World, 1927).

Real Life

_____

"If eight men started from their respective homes in New Orleans, Dallas, Omaha, Minneapolis, Toronto, New York City, Charleston, and Jacksonville, and travelled by the shortest and quickest routes until they met, they would shake hands 16½ yards north of the Custom House on Fourth Street, Louisville, on a sewer cap, midway between a trolley pole and a fire plug."[1]

NOTE
1. *Caron's City Directory* (Louisville, 1926), p. 83.

Main Chance

MON·FEB·14·1927
LOUISVILLE·HYDRO·ELECTRIC·Co.
CONSTRUCTION·DEPT.
POWER·HOUSE·INTERIOR·FROM·NORTH·END
Photo·No·79472

71659

Athlete – 1

Actors – 5

Actress – 1

Agents – 14

Attorneys – 37

Accountants – 16

Apprentice – 1

Auto Dealers – 8

Attendants – 2

Auditors – 7

Advertising Men – 8

Auctioneer – 1

Army Officer – 1

Aviators – 3

Awning Worker – 1

Artists – 5

Assemblers – 3

Architects – 5

Barbers – 89

Boilermakers – 41

Butlers – 6

Bartenders – 6

Bricklayers – 48

Baseball Player – 1

Butchers – 66

Bakers – 65

Brokers – 17

Bankers – 12

Blacksmiths – 26

Bookkeepers – 27

Buyers – 3

Brick Masons – 2

Beauty Parlor
      Operators – 3

Bookbinders – 2

Belter – 1

Bill Poster – 1

Baggage Men – 2

Broom Makers – 5

Bondsmen – 2

Bus Boys – 2

Box Makers – 8

Bridge Men – 9

Brass Workers – 3

Bellhops – 8

Bootblacks – 7

Backer – 1

Battery Man – 1

Brakeman – 1

Bus Owner – 1

Can Makers – 2

Checkers – 3

Carpenters – 221

Chauffeurs – 840

Cooks – 118

Cleaners – 18

Concrete Workers – 32

Coal Dealers – 9

Contractors – 93

Clerks – 604

Collectors – 28

Cabinet Makers – 17

Cigar Makers – 2

Cotton Mill Worker – 1

Candy Makers – 8

Civil Engineers – 3

Car Washers – 2

Conductors – 2

Crane Operators – 4

Capitalists – 2

Credit Man – 1

Casket Maker – 1

Cutters – 6

Constables – 3

Circulators – 4

Core Makers – 3

Cable Worker – 1

Coopers – 23

Chemists – 2

Car Repairers – 2

Chicken Picker – 1

Cashiers – 3

Cap Maker – 1

Circus Performer – 1

Crater – 1

Chef – 1

Carpet Layer – 1

Coast Guard – 1

Detectives – 2

Dispenser – 1

Dairy Men – 7

Delivery Boys – 6

Draftsmen – 5

Dishwashers – 19

Druggists – 18

Decorators – 20

Doctors – 51

Dentists – 7

Dressmakers – 2

Dry Kiln Operator – 1

Dancer – 1

Distiller – 1
Drillers – 8
Designers – 8
Doll Makers – 5
Dispatchers – 2
Director – 1
Deputy Sheriffs – 5

Engineers – 66
Electricians – 80
Elevator Operators – 8
Enamelers – 31
Embalmers – 2
Expressmen – 21
Editor – 1
Engravers – 3
Etcher – 1
Examiner – 1

Financiers – 2
Farmers – 186
Firemen – 62
Foremen – 47
Finishers – 11
Florists – 15
Fruit Dealers – 8

Fishermen – 2
Furriers – 2
Furnace Men – 2
Floor Lady – 1
Furniture Finisher – 1
Fortune Teller – 1

Gardeners – 17
Garage Men – 14
Grinders – 4
Grocers – 39
Glazers – 6
Game Warden – 1
Glue Man – 1
Glass Cutter – 1
Groom – 1
Glass Grinder – 1
Glass Blower – 1
Graders – 2
Grave Diggers – 2
Gas Fitter – 1
Golf Course Tender – 1
Glass Worker – 1
Guards – 2

Housekeepers – 1161

Hod Carriers – 18
Hucksters – 16
Hostlers – 8
Houseworkers – 52
Helpers – 55
Horsemen – 17
Harness Makers – 3
Hair Dressers – 3
Hotel Proprietors – 4

Insurance Agents – 68
Ice Men – 30
Iron Workers – 69
Inspectors – 22
Investigators – 2
Interns – 2
Ice Cream Makers – 2
Interior Decorator – 1

Janitors – 74
Junk Dealers – 14
Jockeys – 20
Janitress – 1
Jumper – 1
Jeweler – 1

Lumber Graders – 4
Laborers – 6144
Laundry Men – 21
Laundresses – 68
Lumber Men – 2
Linemen – 19
Latherers – 9
Linotype Operators – 2

Mechanics – 368
Machinists – 152
Merchants – 306
Molders – 53
Manufacturers – 21
Maids – 33
Manicurists – 2
Maintenance Man – 1
Managers – 82
Musicians – 35
Marines – 2
Millwrights – 79
Motormen – 14
Metal Finishers – 50
Movers – 8
Mail Carriers – 4
Messengers – 9

Marble Setters – 2	Printers – 78	Private Policemen – 3	Stone Masons – 20
Miners – 18	Painters – 338	Panel Setter – 1	Shoemakers – 30
Miller – 1	Plumbers – 86	Park Guard – 1	Seamstresses – 12
Milk Men – 3	Paper Hangers – 95	Pottery Worker – 1	Steel Workers – 7
Milliners – 2	Porters – 141	Prohibition Agent – 1	Stenographers – 15
Ministers – 4	Peddlers – 195		Salesladies – 11
Moving Picture Operator – 1	Polishers – 8	Realtors – 66	Stucco Worker – 1
Missionary Worker – 1	Pool Room Operators – 36	Railroaders – 107	Spooler – 1
Mail Clerks – 3	Plasterers – 53	Restaurant Proprietors – 48	Steam Shovel Operators – 3
Metal Heater – 1	Promotor – 1	Retired – 6	Show Girl – 1
	Piano Tuner – 1	Repair Men – 17	Secretaries – 7
Newspapermen – 40	Pianist – 1	Representative – 1	Stage Hands – 3
Newsboys – 24	Professors – 2	Rescue Workers – 2	Supervisors – 2
Nurses – 12	Pressers – 48	Riggers – 2	Sign Painters – 9
	Pipe Fitters – 18	Radio Experts – 4	Sawyers – 20
Operators – 20	Prostitutes – 711	Riveter – 1	Sailors – 8
Organist – 1	Proprietors – 14	Rooming House	Soldiers – 33
Orderlies – 3	Pawn Broker – 1	Proprietors – 22	Soft Drink Stand
Oil Promoters – 2	Paper Cleaner – 1	Reporters – 3	Operators – 23
Oil Tester – 1	Press Feeders – 2	Race Track Men – 4	Service Station
Organ Maker – 1	Preachers – 10		Operators – 14
Opticians – 5	Photographers – 4	Showmen – 5	Superintendents – 18
	Pin Boys – 2	Sheetmetal Workers – 30	Specialty Man – 1
Packers – 5	Pavers – 3	Salesmen – 828	Section Hand – 1
Perfume Maker – 1	Postmaster – 1	Students – 483	Stockers – 2
Pugilists – 9	Produce Man – 1	Steamfitters – 18	Shirt Cutter – 1

School Teachers — 4	Tool Makers — 3	Telephone Operators — 9	Warden — 1
Saddler — 1	Trimmers — 3		Washerwoman — 1
Shipping Clerks — 4	Truckers — 79	Ushers — 3	Window Trimmer — 1
Stable Men — 8	Tuck Pointer — 1	Umbrella Repairers — 2	Welders — 15
Steeple Jacks — 4	Tent Maker — 1	Upholsterers — 8	Waiters — 96
Stock Men — 2	Tobacco Workers — 183	Undertakers — 4	Waitresses — 29
Switchman — 1	Teamsters — 83		Woodworkers — 37
Storekeeper — 1	Tinners — 29	Vulcanizers — 2	Well Digger — 1
Stone Cutters — 2	Tailors — 35	Varnish Maker — 1	Watch Repairer — 1
Soda Dispenser — 1	Tire Service Men — 11	Varnish Rubbers — 3	Warehouse Man — 1
Steam Boatmen — 9	Typist — 1	Valet — 1	Weavers — 6
Scrub Woman — 1	Truck Drivers — 89	Veterinarian — 1	Waxer — 1
Solicitors — 5	Taxi Drivers — 39		Wood Turner — 1
	Tile Setters — 9	Water Boy — 1	
Tunnel Worker — 1	Teachers — 8	Watchmen — 12	Yard Man — 1
Title Examiner — 1	Tree Surgeons — 5	Window Washer — 1	
Transfer Men — 4	Tester — 1	Watch Makers — 5	No Occupation — 1034
Trunk Makers — 2	Timekeepers — 4	Writer — 1	Unknown — 1822[1]

NOTE
1. Louisville Department of Police, *1928 Annual Report.*

"Dear Miss Grey: We are two girls, sixteen years of

age, are considered good-looking and are very attractive. We are thinking of becoming 'movie stars' . . . is it necessary for us to be 'beautiful' and . . . is it very expensive? . . . where should we go and to whom? . . . TWO CUTIES"[1]

"Dear Miss Grey: I am a young girl, seventeen, and I am sorry to say I was foolish enough to henna my hair. Now I would like to know the quickest and best way to make it the natural shade. (2) I have traveled everywhere, and for some reason I am unhappy. About a year ago I was a very popular young lady and dressed attractively. Now my father cannot afford to give me the things I used to have and . . . I am at a standstill . . . have you any suggestions? (3) What do you think of a young man who, after I disappointed him twice, wrote me a very unkind note. Then at the end he wrote: 'I hope this finds you in the best of health. Forgotten as your friend' . . . ? (4) Miss Grey, could I teach dancing? . . . FAVORITE"[2]

"Hollywood, California . . . My Dear Jack: How glad I am to hear from you. Forgive you? Well of course I do! . . . I was as much to blame as you—only too proud to admit it . . . Have learned a lot this past six months . . . Hollywood has taught me a great deal: for one thing it has shown me that I am not such a much as I thought. Oh, how glad I'll be to get back home. I even want a whiff of that old corncob . . . I no longer despise your little old Ford, and the old town doesn't seem such a slow burg . . . As to what I think of you, will tell you more about it under the elm tree on the front lawn . . . MAY"[3]

"Dear Miss Grey: How is it all of the girls I know are popular and always have engagements? I stay in the house every night and read . . . I do not go with anyone as I have been done dirty by several whom I liked . . . I am always lonesome and blue . . . I am twenty-one years old . . . Do you think I will meet a nice man I will care for, as I never like any of them long, as they all want to be familiar and I never cared for that. I like one who shows you he likes you by doing kind things . . . BLUE EYES"[4]

"Dear Miss Grey: Please excuse this stationery, for it is all I have for the present. About a week ago, a boyfriend of mine wrote me a letter . . . The boy has been going with another girl for years . . . I thought they were engaged. He said some things in the letter I did not like. I answered . . . very cool . . . I have never heard from him. I am afraid I have made him mad . . . Whenever I try to do something, it always turns out wrong and I make a fool of myself. I never know when I am doing the right or wrong thing. There is something that tells me to do one thing, and then something tells me to do another . . . I ask other people's advice and when I take it, it turns out wrong . . . I don't want to make a fool of myself . . . it just seems that I can never go with the fellows I want to . . . I get so blue on Sunday evenings when all of my friends have dates . . . I don't try to tell myself I don't care, for down in my heart I do. I am just a plain girl with no attractions or charm whatever. I do want a good time while I am young. A PLAIN GIRL"[5]

"Dear Miss Grey: I met a boy recently that I liked very much and he seemed to care for me, but the first time I had an engagement with him, he took me for a ride in his automobile.

He picked out rather dark roads I thought and stopped several times and put out the lights and because I insisted he drive on he got so ugly that I got out and walked home . . . I know I love this boy, even though I have been with him only one time . . . I am afraid I hurt his feelings. I know I shouldn't have gotten out of the car, but I was uneasy. I know too that a girl should not kiss a boy until she is engaged, but I did it because I love the boy. I just couldn't help it . . ."[6]

"My Dearest . . . When I get back to you, remember I won't take 'No' for an answer—even if you dare suggest it. I love you so terribly—I just have to have you even though it means reverting to cave man stuff. It won't be necessary, will it dearest? . . ."[7]

"Dear Friend,

How are you? I won't say I'am fine as I'am not but there is nothing the matter you know what I mean. Arthur, I hated very much to have to write this as I know you said your mother did [not] like to see so much mail coming to you from me. And I also hated very much to write it, but Mr. Tarence I must see you at as early a date as possible as I wish to ask you something and also to tell you something. Arthur I'am not writing this letter to scare you and hope you don't feel that way. But I must see you . . . Now don't be offended and don't be affraid as accidents often occur in play."[8]

"Dear Miss Grey . . . Do you think there is any harm in going to roadhouses in a party? The men in our crowd are about thirty-five or thirty-six years old. I am twenty-three. Are they too old for me? What do you think of a girl who goes to a roadhouse and gets intoxicated? She was on the dance floor and could hardly stand up . . . The men in our crowd sometimes have highballs and I do not see harm in it if they do not take too much. Do you? All the men drink nowadays it seems. I am

just beginning to get used to it. At first I thought it was terrible . . . I know you do not believe in girls drinking, or staying out late, or kissing boys . . . but . . . what are girls to do? I'm sure I don't want to sit home nights because I won't be sociable . . . PUZZLED ME"[9]

"Dear Miss Grey: I am twenty years old . . . Do you think a man nineteen years my senior too old for me? I have known him five years. I have only gone with him a few times, but he has been to my home repeatedly. Some of my friends tell me I should not go with him, that he is too old. Do you think I should pay any attention to them, if we really love each other? Don't you think I am really old enough to know what I am doing? . . . NOBODY'S DARLING"[10]

"My dear husband:

Hope you are well. Your babie has bin real sick. He is having chills. He feels better now. I wish you could be with us. I haven't got to work now since Wednesday. He won't let me leave him. Hun, I wanted to see you last night. Why was you in such a hurry? I was eating supper when you came and hated to leave the table; so by the time I got through you were gone. Are you mad at me? Hun be careful when you come and watch. I have got something to tell you. You come tonight after they have gone to bed. I leave the bottom door unfastened for you and be awfle careful . . . hun come down about nine or eny time you see a chance to get in without anybody seeing you. Watch and look everywhere. good bye and bring me a sweet kiss good bye,
Your future wife,
Mrs. Ed Harker"[11]

"Dear Miss Grey . . . My daughter and I had an argument as to whether a girl takes a chance in marrying a man who is a poor loser in sports and displays his temper and character by throwing his tennis racquet to the ground when things do not go right. I say I would not take a chance in marrying a man like that . . . MOTHER"[12]

"Dear Miss Grey . . . I have tried everything and failed. I have a daughter, eighteen. She has been going with a young man, twenty-two. I have asked her to give him up as . . . she is too young. I have offered her everything I can think of to leave this boy . . . The boy knows that I do not care for him . . . he comes anyway. I don't want to tell him to stay away . . . My husband does not care for him or like his looks, and since my daughter will not give him up, my husband has made my life miserable and tells me it is my fault . . . I have cried for two weeks and got down on my knees to her . . . [The boy's] salary is very small, and I am afraid they will run away and get married. He has no education . . . I would like her to marry a man with some education, and . . . some kind of position . . . BROKEN HEARTED MOTHER"[13]

"They were carrying on and telling the Police that I was a gentile and that he was a Jew, and that we could not live together, and Zeitelson and Hanna were also out there telling the Police, and the Police wanted to know what was their objection, and they said they can't live together because she was gentile and he was Jew, we are not going to let them live together, and the Police ordered them to move away and let me alone . . . she told me how dreadful it was that Joe should have married out of his religion and her grandfather was such a religious man, that he was a Rabbi and people believed so in him, and I said, Hanna my people were good Catholics as yours are Jews, I feel that we should have married if we loved one another, regardless of religion or anything, and she said Joe cheated me and them and everything, and cried and went on and I don't know what all."[14]

————————————————

"Dear Miss Grey: I am twenty-four and considered good-looking, educated, and clever. I am a stylish dresser because I can afford to dress well. I hold the position of secretary and have many girlfriends. But the trouble is this: I cannot . . . interest a young man . . . to be serious with me. I go out a great deal to dances with girls and I meet many young men. They tell me I am interesting and clever. [They] spend the evening with me, take me home, ask for my phone number, and I never hear from them again . . . ALMOST AN OLD MAID"[15]

"Dear Miss Grey: I am twenty-six years old and love a young man two years my senior employed by the same firm. I have been working for this firm four years as a stenographer, and the young man has been with them much longer. He has never asked me to go out with him. I know nothing about him except in a business way. Does real love exist in a case like this . . . ?"[16]

"Dear Mabel . . . your sweet face gets between me and . . . my ledger; your golden curls seem tangled in the . . . column of figures, and I caught myself today addressing an old respected customer as 'Pet.' It is no use! . . . you must set the day. I cannot have you interfering with my business in this manner . . . When you are once my own, I may, in the consciousness of possession, regain my usual business habits. Ever yours. George"[17]

"Dear Miss Grey: I am twenty and have a father and mother dependent on me. I earn a good salary in a business, thanks to the manager, whom I love. This man is thirty, seems to be happily married, and tells me he loves me . . . When I tell him he should think of his wife, and that I think it is wrong to allow him to meet me evenings, he always says he loves me too much to give me up. Is there no way out of this? . . . ANX-IOUS"[18]

"Now that you have been appointed to the official position where no woman can accompany you, and your fortune is assured, I shout with joy at your success and weep in silence over the thought that our marriage will again be postponed one year . . . I laugh, and yet the laugh does not ring clear—it is . . . full of tears . . . This year means . . . to you . . . excitement, prominence, and fortune—to me, it means restlessness, dreariness, and sobbing . . . At night, as I gaze on my trousseau trunk, I fear lest all will be ruined; as I remove the dainty garments one by one, they are drenched with tears of joy . . ."[19]

"Dear Miss Grey: Two years ago, when eighteen, I met a man of twenty-three. He was not wealthy, and our friendship continued for a year. He realized he loved me. We then had a talk, in which he said poverty and love would not harmonize, so we parted . . . I became engaged to another man . . . Last month, I met the first man accidentally, and discovered I couldn't continue with the other. The engagement was broken, but that is not all. The first man knows I am free again, but still he insists it would be cowardly to make me suffer by going through hardship. Is there anything a girl with a little pride can do to make him see things in a different light? JOY"[20]

"My dear: Just received the letter from your attorney . . . it was no surprise to me as I have felt for some time that you really did not wish a reconciliation, but wanted your freedom . . . your sudden leap to wealth is the cause of all the trouble . . . I feel you want a new wife to match the new home, the new furniture, the new cars, and all of the other new things . . . I cannot forget the years we spent together in poverty and love . . . Dickey dear . . ."[21]

"Dear Miss Grey . . . I am very unhappy . . . I have only been married five months . . . Before we were married, [my husband] made a real pal of me and I was always his joy. After we were married, it seemed as though he confided his business matters and accepted his family's advice in preference to mine, even though I continue to work and help him in money matters, then when I tell him where he might save a nickle or a dime, he gets very cross with me, saying he is disgusted and tired of everything. He never was cross with me til his family mixed in his business. They treat me very nice.

"I cry most every day because I have lost confidence in my husband. I wanted to make so much out of my married life and make him just as happy as he did me, but now it is so hard for me to keep him from knowing I'm so unhappy. I do love him, but it was so different then, when I had all the confidence. I'm not tired of him, but he has almost made me lose interest in life. Because when I love, it is so deep, and he is the only man I ever loved sincerely . . . I gave up pleasure for him. I have chances every day to trifle on him, but I'm true blue and he knows I am. I have so often tried to figure out whose fault it is. I work every day and keep house . . . I'm losing weight, and no one knows but myself . . . BILLY"[22]

38

BURLESQUE AT POPULAR PRICES
TWICE DAILY
MATINEE 2 15
FREDERICK LA PLANO
"Cut A Woman In Two"
THESE SAWS USED BY Prof. LA PLANO
IN "CUTTING A WOMAN IN TWO"
AT EVERY PERFORMANCE
IF YOU DOUBT THEM
BRING YOUR OWN SAW
ALL THIS WEEK
ALL THIS WEEK
COURTESY
BONAR-SUMMERS HOWE CO.
BOX OFFICE NOW OPEN
MATINEE TO DAY 2 15 P.M.

"While I was carrying my baby I was sick most of the

time and couldn't eat everything, and he refused to buy me things that I craved, such as watermelon, peaches, and things like that. The baby was born on the seventh of January, 1922, and died on the tenth of January, 1922. When the child was born, I was so torn that it was necessary for the doctor to take several stitches—this caused by his failure to call the doctor in time. When it was time for the baby to be born, and I took sick, he wouldn't call the doctor. I begged and begged him to do so, and he waited to call him for such a long time that I almost died . . . The morning after the baby was born he cursed and abused me, and twelve days after the birth of my child, January 19, 1922, he had intercourse with me which broke the stitches that were taken in me at the time of the birth of my child, and caused me to flood, and I got so weak I couldn't put up with it anymore. The last few nights that I stayed with him I was almost scared to death. I looked to be killed before morning—he threatened my life, threatened to shoot me. He just got mad at me and cursed me and said if I ever left him he would kill me."[23]

"At his mother's suggestion, he quit showing me any consideration whatever, never kissed me or caressed me and knowing that I was anxious to have children he had promised me that it would not be long before I had a child but his mother convinced him that he did not want any children so he told me that if I ever had a child he would leave me, but this threat was not necessary as after going to live with his mother he practically quit living with me as man and wife. I believe that this was his mother's wish, for her room and the one occupied by the defendant and myself was joined by large sliding doors and she insisted on these doors being left open at night, saying that there was 'no reason in the world why they should not be left wide open' between the two rooms and from the time we retired until we got up the following morning she would come back and forth through our bedroom at least six times when she could have easily gone through the hall."[24]

"Dear Miss Grey . . . I have been married three years to one of the best husbands and have a little girl two years old. Before the baby came, my mother-in-law was very good to me, but since baby came, she thinks I should let her have sole control . . . When I correct the baby for anything, she says it don't hurt for her to do that and to leave her alone. She always pets the baby and tells her to talk back to 'mammy' when I scold baby . . . I am just so discouraged . . . my husband . . . says I am the most to blame. I am twenty years old but he says I am too young to know. He told me before we were married that as soon as he was able we would go to housekeeping, and I know he is not trying. He bought a nice big car, and one of the best radio sets . . . I tried to get him to put the money in a home . . . I just can't live with his mother much longer . . . I want him to let me and baby go back to my mother's . . . I tell him our separation is coming closer and closer . . . JIMMIE"[25]

"Dear Miss Grey: We have been married five years and I find that I don't love my husband as I once did. Instead of that, I keep thinking of my old beau who is still single. I have no children; would it be wrong to tell my husband how things are? UNHAPPY"[26]

"I was conductor and Carl Meaney was motorman . . . she boarded the car at the front vestibule where Meaney the motorman was, and we had a ten minute lay-over there and

Bettie Mott and Carl Meaney had intercourse right there in the car while I kept watch for them . . . She would give him money and say: 'Here is some money for you sweetie, go get you something with it. You are the best Daddy in the world.' . . . I have heard her make a good many slurry remarks about her husband. She would say that there was not a good jazz in her husband and that his ass reminded her of two coffee grains tacked on a board."[27]

"Dear little Sweetheart: Well Bud came in last night after I came home baby I sure am disgusted—well they are trying to make me go back with him tonight—oh I am so afraid that they will make me go. I don't know what to do—now Sweetie don't let no one around here see you no place I don't know how I can get out to meet you or anything. You know I told you I loved you well dear I certainly do—so write me a note and leave it with Lucile what to do excuse bad writing as I am in a hurry—with lots of love Emma I never done what you told me not to"[28]

"That woman has made life a perfect Hell on earth for me. She has thrown dishes from the top of the steps to the bottom and she has broken things up all over my house. She hit me in the head with a silver pitcher at one time and made a gash in my head because I wanted the window up a little too far and she wanted it down . . . " Q: "Is she a drug fiend? . . . " A: "She used to take three things . . . Paraldhyde was one and another was chloral and now it is called under the trade name of—wait a minute now—bromidia. Those are the two and the other was morphine . . . When my wife was herself she could be very agreeable at times, but when she got full of this paraldhyde I would come in and find her lying on the floor apparently in a stupor and put her in bed and at other times she would rage and walk up and down and at other times she would lock herself in her room . . . "[29]

"Dear Miss Grey: I have been married ten years, and my husband has become infatuated with another woman. He wants a divorce . . . What would you advise me to do? Also, do you think it would be proper for a woman of twenty-six, about five feet six inches in height, to bob her hair? And please publish a recipe for butterscotch pie. BLACK EYED SUSIE"[30]

"He went away last summer and was gone and stayed away until Christmas—I was cleaning out his room and I found at least forty half pint whiskey bottles . . . in his table drawer and in his reading desk and in his chest of drawers where he keeps his clothes and in his closet—you could find them everywhere . . . all I have left to keep me from the poor house in my old age is this property down in Florida . . . he refused to sign the deed and waited and was trying to hold myself and my sister up when the property was ours, he had nothing to do with it,—we wanted to sell it while the place was booming down there and the prices were good, we didn't want to wait until it was just a sand pile . . . "[31]

"Although he knew I knew he was intimate with the housekeeper, and was practically living in adultery with her in my own house, and presence, he insisted upon keeping her in my house, feeding her at my table, and forcing me to live with a woman whom I knew to be his mistress, and taking her each morning to work with him at his office, she sitting in the front seat of his car with him . . . he would go out three and four times a week, and my housekeeper would go out on the same nights, and he would come home at twelve and one o'clock and she would come in within ten, twenty, or thirty minutes after he did."[32]

STEWART'S

"Well, the first time he mistreated me was when I had my hair bobbed, I had my hair bobbed and came home and when he saw that I had my hair bobbed he got mad and grabbed me by the head and jerked me around and jerked me by the hair and I begged him to please take his hands off of me and then he went out and got drunk that night and they brought him home dead drunk and laid him in the bed and he vomited all over the floor and then the next day or so he threw me down over his lap and whipped me until it just burned—it burned so that I couldn't sit down for a couple of days and then he wouldn't speak to me for a week and that finally accumulated into a quarrel and he blamed me for the whole thing, he said that I would not give into his demands, on this occasion, about three o'clock in the morning he woke me up and wanted to have intercourse with me and I didn't feel like doing it and he got mad and swore, he would quarrel about things like that—he said if I had given into his demands at that time everything would have been all right, that our whole quarrel would have been over but I just didn't feel like it . . . when I was not a wife to him as often as he wanted me to, he would get mad, if I would be a wife to him once a day he wanted it twice and if I was a wife to him twice then he would want it three times, and if I didn't do it when he wanted me to, why then he was abusive and would not speak to me and was sullen and mean the whole time and sometimes he would not even sit down and eat the meals I would cook for him."[33]

"Most of the quarrels were caused by the fact that at night he would want me to undress before him and expose my person; I would not do it, for I thought there was no reason because I was married that I need not display any modesty, and I felt that I was entitled to privacy about some things and would undress modestly and as privately as I could, and that would start a quarrel, and he would lay all night fussing and quarreling about it; there was about two years that I never closed an eye until three or four o'clock in the morning and I just couldn't stand it. He complained that I was not affectionate, well he was not clean and has gone from ten weeks to three months without taking a bath; then he was at one time affected with a loathsome disease and of course I was not affectionate with him; and he would have vermin on him and would not clean himself up nor take care of his person and would want me to sleep with him and be affectionate toward him and I just couldn't do it."[34]

"He would insist on having sexual intercourse with me every night, and also during periods of menstruation. When I was menstruating, I would refuse, and he would pack his grip and say that he was going to the YMCA to spend the night. In order to keep peace and get along with him, I would yield to his desires. It affected my health, and I was forced to get Dr. George Boon to administer medical treatment."[35]

"He is very immoral and has exposed himself immorally any number of times in front of people. He has stood in the front door (I hate to tell this, because it seems so terrible to me) and has shaken his parts at women as they passed on the street and he has been arrested twice for doing this and for insulting women as they walked along in front of the house. Why the neighbors could not sit out in front on account of his immoral conduct . . . He is not a drinking man, and that is what makes it so much worse, because if he did drink, a person would blame it on the booze. I really cannot understand him."[36]

"I was compelled to take in roomers to try to make a living. I had three Mexican boarders and my husband accused me of being intimate with them, which was wholly without foundation. In connection with our married relations, instead of having intercourse in the natural form, he wanted to have intercourse with me by way of his mouth. I told him I could not stand for anything like this, and he told me if I did not, he would get somebody that did, and I told him to go ahead and do it. He tried to make me think that all married people did that, and as I was only fifteen years old when I married him, I really did not know whether this was so or not."[37]

"He was rough and cruel to me at nights in his personal habits. He knew that he caused a tumor on me on account of his rough animal passions, and he didn't seem to have any respect for me or how much pain it caused me right while that tumor was so bad so long as he could satisfy his animal passions."[38]

"He cursed me and beat me. Yes sir, he did, he threatened me with all kinds of bodily harm. And he ran me off from home. And said he didn't care any more for me. And just a few days before I left he beat me, and said he didn't care any more for me. It was just because I got a little black on his hand when he was sitting in front of the fire. He was awful particular about his hands. He worked in the store. He worked in the Five and Ten Cent Store. He was awful particular about his hands."[39]

"If I would not get up at five or six o'clock in the morning to open up his business, while he laid in bed, he had a big whip there which he bought to use on the dog, and he beat me with that whip unmercifully which caused me to be confined to my bed for three or four days. Last May, 1923, when I was pregnant, the defendant came home drunk . . . he pushed me down the steps, which caused me to have a miscarriage, which nearly cost me my life. When there would be anybody around and he could not mistreat me otherwise, he would burn me with cigarettes and tramp on my feet . . . He would get telephone calls every day, three or four calls, for him to call a certain woman. My cousin . . . was in the store one night when the telephone rang and my cousin answered the telephone and a woman asked for Mr. Norris and this woman said, 'Are you going to see me again tonight? . . . believe me you had better bring those things you use'

"One morning, the defendant came home in a drunken condition, he sneaked in the house and turned on the light. I kept calling him and he continued to turn the light on and off. Finally I got up and he was hiding in a corner of the room with a knife in his hand, with which he intended to kill me."[40]

———————————————

Dr. Lewis began the New Year of 1918 by having too much to drink at the Magnolia Gardens. A waiter had him taken home in a taxi. The next morning, when the doctor woke up, he noticed that his wife was kneeling in front of their bedroom sofa with her arms stretched out and a marble table top on her head. After he went down to check the furnace, he examined her and concluded she'd died of diabetes.

When the police came, he explained that someone had assaulted and killed her while he'd been asleep. "She was certainly a good-looking woman," he said. The police asked him why the collie, who slept at the foot of the bed, hadn't woken him up. He explained that the animal had been doing a lot of sleeping lately, and wasn't such a dependable watchdog. He also said that he'd been doing a lot of sleeping himself because of the morphine he was in the habit of taking for his neuritis.

Mrs. Lewis looked like she'd been hit between the eyes before she'd been strangled. The doctor said that she'd probably fallen down and hurt herself, since she was a heavy drinker and used to do things like that all the time.

The police began looking for motives. Captain Brown said that a year before, a woman who was a relative of Mrs. Lewis's had come to him with the story that Dr. Lewis had tried to choke her. The dead woman's half-brother, who was the director of a sanatorium for drug addicts, said that his sister had never touched a drop. Meanwhile, Dr. Lewis was in jail, begging for an injection of "dope" — to clear his mind, he said — and telling everyone who'd listen that the black gardener had done it all. The coroner's jury indicted him when detectives found a pan of bloody rags under the bathtub and a bloody towel in the closet.

Hundreds of curious people came to the funeral home to get a look at Mrs. Lewis. Three of the dead woman's sisters came to town. They said the man was a beast who was always threatening to kill the poor woman every time they came to visit.

Dr. Lewis's lawyer argued that he was insane. Dr. Edwin Bruce testified that Lewis was a drug addict who had been under the influence of alcohol and morphine. He said he'd known him for fourteen years. Dr. Alex Griswald testified that he'd treated him for syphilis, but that Lewis hadn't believed it. Griswald said that Lewis's brain had been damaged by drugs and disease. He said he was a moral pervert who didn't know the difference between right and wrong. The jury sent him off to the asylum.

Five years later, the doctor became sane enough to be tried again.[41]

Minnie Blackerby was a married woman.

She worked in a department store to make a little extra money and pass the time. One day, a man came in to buy some sheets. A few days later, he came back for something else. He said he was a dentist named Charlie Heavrin. He offered to examine her mouth. He thought she might need some cavities filled. She did. She needed so much work that every time she came for an appointment, Charlie put a sign on his door that said he was out. She used to bring him presents. One was a box of cigars with a poem on the lid. "Here is the man who's fifty/Just in his prime/Improved with age/Like rare old wine/For a man that age/Can love so well/He makes one forget/There is a hell." When she couldn't come to the office, Charlie visited her at a house she owned. One of her tenants remembered how Charlie touched her while she sat on a lounge in the front room, dressed in a "short gown." Charlie told Lola, his receptionist, that he had "a million-dollar baby" and "a hundred-thousand-dollar doll" who was going to buy him a limousine. He told Lola she could wave to him when he went by.

Minnie's husband wasn't a millionaire. He was a tobacco broker who didn't trust her. He put a jack on her home phone so he could listen to her call the dentist. He heard things like Charlie asking Minnie what she had on, and Minnie telling Charlie "a blue kimono and velvet slippers." He heard so much that one day, when Minnie was at the dentist's office, he knocked as loud as he could on the door and then asked to have his teeth cleaned. The doctor came out and told him he was busy. He went across the street until his wife walked out, then he took her back in. He told Heavrin he wanted to have a talk. They had a fight and he killed the dentist.

During his trial, he denied he'd said some of the things that were written in the confession he made to the police. He didn't say the police lied. All he said was that the stenographer had kept falling asleep. The judge called the stenographer, who denied ever having taken a nap in his long career. He told the court that he'd taken depositions in 100 of the 118 countries of the state. The judge reminded him that there were 120. Everyone laughed. Blackerby got twenty-one years.[42]

Cecil Wells was a rich, thirty-three-year-old commodities broker.

He was killed by Edward Humphrey, twenty-nine, a boyhood friend, former employee, and traveling companion after Wells tried to castrate him. Wells kidnapped Humphrey and took him to a rented house in the black ghetto. After he had tied him, spread-eagled, to the floor of a bedroom, he chloroformed him and took his pants off. The room was equipped with a set of surgical instruments, rubber sheets, a hatchet, and several large fruit boxes. Wells intended to castrate Humphrey, chop him up, wrap him in sheets, stuff him in the fruit boxes, and send him off to Mercer, Wisconsin, where the two of them had gone camping.

Humphrey and Wells had known one another since they were twelve. Humphrey had known Wells's wife, Jeannine, for ten years. She had married Wells when she was fifteen. After Humphrey got out of the army in 1919, Wells gave him a job buying and selling sugar and beans. Three years later, Wells accused him of seducing his wife. Humphrey denied it; Wells punched him in the face. Humphrey quit his job and moved to Detroit. Wells apologized. He asked Humphrey to help find the men who were really guilty: the ones who had tried it when he and Jeannine were on their Florida vacation. Humphrey agreed. Wells made the plans; Humphrey bought the guns. They traveled to New Orleans, Houston, Tampa, Jacksonville, and Lake City, South Carolina. In Lake City, they paid a girl to lure the sheriff into the woods, where they tied and beat him. In Houston, they posed as rich oil investors and persuaded a man to drive them into the country to show them an oil lease. They treated him just like the sheriff. Wells said he'd spent $75,000 to get even.

During Christmas, 1923, Wells told his wife that he was going to teach Humphrey a lesson. He went to Chicago to ask a black doctor if he would castrate an imaginary idiot cousin. When the man refused, he asked another black doctor in Louisville to do the same thing. When the man in Louisville refused, he bought his own surgical instruments. He read medical texts and studied hypnosis with the president of a dry cleaning firm. He told his wife that he was going to cripple Humphrey for life. He took a few shots at her in their bedroom; she swore that she loved him. He went back to Chicago to hire a lady detective to watch her. Then he stopped in Indianapolis to talk an out-of-work truck driver who said he was a private detective into coming to Louisville to guard his warehouse from an imaginary thief.

One day in March, he asked Humphrey to stop by the warehouse after work. That same day, he asked an old high-school friend who was an organist in a movie theater to help him teach someone a lesson. When Humphrey walked into the office, the truck driver from Indianapolis thought he was the thief that Wells had hired him to catch. They handcuffed him and threw him into a car. The organist was waiting outside and followed them. The three of them hauled Humphrey into the bedroom and tied him down. Three days later, Wells's wife went to the rented house. Wells came downstairs to talk to her. When he went up again, Humphrey asked him to let him go to the toilet. As soon as as he was free, he shot Wells in the chest with a derringer he had hidden in his vest pocket. He ran down the stairs and out the door. A jury acquitted him a week later.[43]

———————————

A woman named Lillian fell in love with a thief named Tex Walters. He used to hypnotize her. The first time was three months after her baby died. He told her she was getting "sleepier and sleepier." She said she closed her eyes and saw her baby "which I loved so much . . . My will became weak but my love became strong." A month later, he hypnotized her again. "I saw a girl, a beautiful girl, the girl whom Tex was to have married . . . She came to kill me and it fright-

ened me . . . but I could not resist him."

When Tex killed a man in a robbery in the city, they sent him to the state penitentiary for life. He asked Lillian to get him out. She bought guns. Tex and two of his friends—Lawrence Griffith and Harry Ferland—tried to shoot their way out. They killed three guards, but didn't get any farther than the mess hall. National Guard troops shot out whole sections of the walls with machine gun volleys, and fired rifle grenades through the windows. Sharpshooters blew holes in shadows. It went on for five days. Then they filled the hall with ammonia gas and stormed it. That's when they discovered that they'd been shooting at corpses. Tex died of wounds he'd gotten in the fight with the guards. Griffith and Ferland died in a double suicide. They'd been dead for four days. They left a message on the back of a bench: "Defiance from death. Remember, you didn't kill us, we killed ourselves . . . If they was ever a game bunch, it's L.G., T.W., H.F." Troops found a note in Tex's pocket. It was to Lillian. "Love to you beloved. I am wounded and surrounded by guards. Goodbye. I will be . . . "[44]

———————————

William Zinmeister ran a soft-drink stand, which was the customary way of selling whisky by the drink. He also took bets.

He'd been married and divorced. He was forty. His former wife had died when her stove exploded. His brother had been sent to prison for life for killing a pregnant woman and her husband in an argument about a ditch. Zinmeister had only two things left: his stand and his daughter Mamie. The police raided the stand even though he paid them off. Then his daughter started going with boys. She was sixteen.

Mamie asked him if she could go to a Sunday church picnic in June. First he said no, then he said yes. A neighbor, who worked at the Ford plant, heard him talking to a customer at the stand. "I'm going to put them off, and if I do, they aren't going to put me in the shape my brother's in . . . I'm going to put myself off." He was cleaning two guns.

He took a taxi out to the picnic. It was at a campground on the river, a few miles from where his brother had gotten into the argument with the man and his wife. He walked up to his daughter who was sitting on the bank, talking with two other girls. He shot her in the face, then leaned over and shot her in the side of the head. One of the girls jumped fifteen feet into the river. He fired and missed her. The other girl ran along the bank. He shot her in the thigh. He walked along, keeping pace with a boy who was swimming away, downstream. He told him he was going to kill him for going with his daugher. The boy said he didn't know her. Zinmeister shot him three times. The boy pulled himself onto the shore, but he didn't shoot him again. "I'll let you go if you're a good boy." He stopped to reload. A young man ran out of the water and up the bank at him. He pulled Zinmeister down, grabbed his gun, threw it in the river, and ran. Zinmeister pulled another gun out of his pants and shot him in the shoulder.

Zinmesiter kept on walking downstream. He walked up to a group of campers with the gun in his hand. He said he'd just killed four people and needed a drink. "This'll be my last hour and my last drink." They ran. A half-hour later, a farmer and his son saw a man running and stumbling through their field. They thought he was a lunatic who'd escaped from the state asylum. By the time they got near him, Zinmeister had caught himself in some barbed wire. They watched him put a gun to his head and blow his brains out. His mother came to the farm to identify him. "Well, let them take him in and bury him. He had a nice home on Sixth Street." Then she turned to the crowd and said, "This ought to be a lesson to every one of you." She pointed at him and said, "That's whisky—nothing but whisky."[45]

Notes

1. "Cynthia Grey's Letters," daily column, Louisville *Herald*, January 24, 1923.
2. "Cynthia Grey," February 17, 1924.
3. "My Old Love Letters," Sunday feature column, Louisville *Herald*, September 2, 1923.
4. "Cynthia Grey," February 17, 1924.
5. "Cynthia Grey," March 3, 1924.
6. "Cynthia Grey," September 23, 1923.
7. "My Old Love Letters," November 11, 1923.
8. Jefferson County Court, Civil Case #131368, 1922.
9. "Cynthia Grey," May 11, 1924.
10. "Cynthia Grey," March 18, 1924.
11. Civil Case #122758, 1921.
12. "Cynthia Grey," August 19, 1923.
13. "Cynthia Grey," August 7, 1923.
14. Civil Case #131438, 1922.
15. "Cynthia Grey," April 20, 1924.
16. "Cynthia Grey," May 4, 1924.
17. "My Old Love Letters," July 1, 1923.
18. "Cynthia Grey," July 1, 1923.
19. "My Old Love Letters," September 23, 1923.
20. "Cynthia Grey," May 11, 1924.
21. "My Old Love Letters," October 14, 1923.
22. "Cynthia Grey," May 20, 1923.
23. Civil Case #129196, 1922.
24. Civil Case #134388, 1922.
25. "Cynthia Grey," May 29, 1924.
26. "Cynthia Grey," November 27, 1924.
27. Civil Case #148116, 1923.
28. Caufield and Shook Photographic Copy #32213.
29. Civil Case #127960, 1921.
30. "Cynthia Grey," August 12, 1923.
31. Civil Case #155413, 1925.
32. Civil Case #156585, 1925.
33. Civil Case #159102, 1925.
34. Civil Case #122571, 1919.
35. Civil Case #144521, 1924.
36. Civil Case #137919 (divorce), 1924.
37. Civil Case #128060, 1921.
38. Civil Case #142425, 1924.
39. Civil Case #158992, 1925.
40. Civil Case #148097, 1924.
41. *Herald*, September 17, 1923, front page; January 2, 1918, front page.
42. *Herald*, March 23, 1923, front page.
43. *Herald*, March 9–18, 1924, front page. Fictitious names have been used in this episode.
44. *Herald*, October 4–8, 1923, front page; December 12, 1923, front page.
45. *Herald*, June 25, 1923.

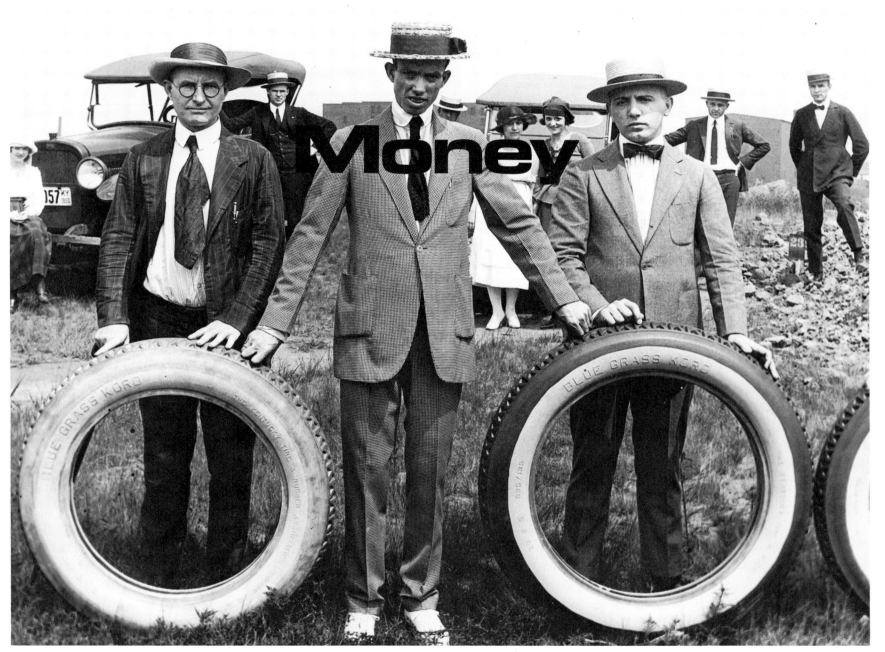

"I came . . . to Louisville with no job in view . . . I started

with an office supply company, but couldn't make enough. I had a wife and child. I tried selling calendars and advertising for a national concern, but my selling experience and ability were not equal to the occasion. I took on a temporary, but secret, investigative accounting job. This was from a firm where a high official had gone wrong. I proved the case, but then we were both out of a job. It took about six months . . .

"A friend of mine recommended me for another accounting job. The pay was fairly good, but I didn't like the type of business. It just didn't suit my taste. Between you and I, it was a casket company.

"A young man called me up and asked me to be his accountant . . . He and two other young men had started a very small manufacturing wholesale business. They kept books wholly by memos, thrown into a large basket. Could I open up a set of books for them? The pay was small. Nothing. Absolutely nothing. But they wanted to incorporate and would pay me in stock, in the new company. I had nothing to lose . . . I kept their books for about three years. At night and odd times.

"An older man, with two sons and a daughter, all past twenty-one . . . bought into the company. This was done on the condition that his three offspring would be given jobs in the plant. It could have worked out fine, if they would have been content to work as regular employees—but no; their daddy was the biggest stockholder by this time and they all wanted to be big chiefs. It became all chiefs and no Indians. Their dad saw how things were going, and decided he wanted out. I could buy him out . . . and if the business failed, I could stop payments and owe him nothing more.

"Of the three original partners, one went on a vacation trip to South America—to the mahogany timberlands on the Amazon. He disappeared and was never heard from again. His family never stopped trying to find him. It ended up with me having 49 percent of the stock and thirty other holding companies having the balance."[1]

Elmer Schmidt and William Werdeman were two young men who were partners in an advertising agency. Times were tough; they needed money. Schmidt convinced Werdeman that the best way to get it was for each to take out an insurance policy and name the other as beneficiary. One of them would drown, the other would collect. Werdeman bought a policy for $7,500; Schmidt told him he already had one for $10,000. As soon as Werdeman had signed, Schmidt offered him a drink. Werdeman took a sip, but wondered if it was poison. Schmidt suggested a card game to decide who would be the lucky man. Schmidt cheated; Werdeman lost. Schmidt said, "Goodbye, my boy. God bless you." Werdeman decided that Schmidt was after his life. He went to the insurance company and canceled the policy. Then he went to the police. The police told him to play along. He went down to the Ohio and left a Palm Beach suit on the bank. The police reported that he'd been plowed under by a speedboat. They registered him in a flophouse under the name of Shawnee Walker, and told him to grow a beard. Three days later, Schmidt went to the insurance company to collect. Werdeman telephoned him and the police listened while Schmidt called him a coward. A week later, they arrested Schmidt. They wanted to know about his other partner, Ed Kearn, who'd disappeared without a trace in 1920.[2]

JUNE 30 1926
LOUISVILLE HYDRO-ELECTRIC CO.
CONSTRUCTION DEPT
FOUNDATION FOR POWER HOUSE
— PHOTO NO 73785 —

In Louisville in 1920, there were two telephone companies. One of them was called the Home Telephone and the other was called the Cumberland. People who subscribed to one couldn't call people who subscribed to the other, and no one could call Cincinnati, St. Louis, or Chicago without a lot of trouble. During the municipal elections of 1921, local business and civic leaders made plans to solve this problem. By 1924, the Home had sold itself to the Cumberland for $6 million, and rates had gone up by an average of 50 percent. This could never have happened without the sincere understanding that local politicians offered local businessmen; nor could it have been achieved without the generous help that the businessmen provided their political colleagues. This was not the first time that there had been such cooperation and understanding in the city, the state, or even the nation. Still, the sale of the Home to the Cumberland deserves to be told again. It is a symmetrical story of men who surrounded themselves with labyrinths of imaginary events.

The chief political agent of the sale was the local Republican party which had come out of the First War with an electoral majority that it held for fourteen years. Chelsey Searcy was the boss. He'd begun his political career at the age of twelve as a precinct worker. He'd been an actor in high school. After two years at Vanderbilt, he came home to read law in the office of a former circuit court judge. He managed two political failures for governor before he found a man who won the Louisville mayor's race in 1917. Once he had his man in office, he had himself appointed chairman of the Sinking Fund, where he collected a salary and administered the city's bonded debt until 1931. He behaved like a game warden: he kept the city's Board of Public Works and Board of Public Safety stocked with political hacks, and the police and the fire departments full of former servicemen who were grateful enough to take orders. He elected his second mayor, named Smith, in 1919, and his third, a man named Huston Quinn, in 1921.[3] Quinn was a chunky version of Herbert Hoover; he had been the city attorney, and was serving as an appeals court judge when Searcy gave him his chance. John Doolan, the Democratic boss, ran a handsome young naval hero named W. Overton Harris against him.

Harris and the Democratic papers, owned by another former judge and mayor named Bingham, did a lot of talking, mostly about how quiet Huston Quinn was. They said that Chelsey Searcy had cut holes in Quinn's back so that he could stick in his fingers and move his head and arms. They said that if Quinn won, the only thing Searcy would let him do was give away the key to the city. They said Searcy was financing the campaign with a $200,000 shake-down of every cop and fireman, and every protected bookie joint, poker club, floating crap game, pool hall, and whisky-selling soft drink stand in the city. Searcy announced that Judge Quinn would not lower himself to make an answer.[4] The accusations continued. The papers charged that city traffic cops worked as lookouts for speakeasies, that the Board of Public Works had spent money on everything but sewers and streets, and that the Republicans had registered more black voters than there were black people in the city. Overton Harris even appealed to "sober, hard-working Negroes" to take a stand against the razor-totting crapshooters that the Republicans were protecting.[5]

The Republicans kept quiet, except for passing out a few pamphlets about how the Democrats were in league with the Pope.[6] Searcy waited until four days before the election; then he had a private meeting with all the smallmouth bass that filled the Board of Public Safety. He warned them that the Democrats had hired some thugs from out-of-town, and were arming 200 "poll-workers" with inch-thick hickory canes. He didn't tell them that 600 of his own men were carrying two-pound brakemen's billies.[7] The night before the election, the head of the Board of Public Safety ordered the police to raid the Democratic headquarters at the Tyler Hotel to arrest the thugs. Instead, the police arrested the Democratic candidate for mayor, the Democratic candidate for sheriff, a Democratic newspaper reporter, the night manager of the hotel, three of his employees, and a few guests. Overton Harris was charged with disorderly conduct, the candidate for sheriff with inciting a riot, and the hotel guests with conspiracy. Mayor Smith came down to the police station to get them out just in time to vote. When it was all over, Quinn got 62,000; Harris got 56,000; thirty-seven people had been arrested; and eleven people, six of them black, had been hospitalized, several of them for acute alcohol poisoning, two of them with wounds suffered when a cop opened up on a crowd of Democrats waiting to vote. The cop shot one man through the lungs, and an old lady in the leg. Most of the people arrested, including the cop, had got into trouble from all the free whisky the Republicans had passed out in the black belt.

66

The primary business agent of the telephone sale was the Cumberland Telephone Company. Its history reads like that of the Carolingian Dynasty. It had gone into business in 1883; it had bought the Great Southern Telephone and Telegraph Company in 1898, the Ohio Valley Telephone and Telegraph Company in 1900, and the East Tennessee Telephone Company in 1912. The same year that it bought the East Tennessee, it itself was bought by American Telephone and Telegraph, controlled by J.P. Morgan, who lived just long enough to sell the Cumberland to South Central Bell for $16 million. When the Cumberland had purchased the Ohio Valley Telephone and Telegraph Company in 1900, it had bought it from a group of Nashville investors, who, in turn, had bought it, a year before, from a Louisville Republican family called the Speeds. The Speeds had sold them the hardware, along with a 200-year franchise that had been granted in 1886 by the Kentucky state legislature. The Louisville Board of Aldermen had agreed to abide by the franchise the Speeds had been granted by the state in 1886; but in 1908, long after the family had sold the Ohio Valley Company to the Nashville group, who had in turn sold it to the Cumberland, the Louisville Board of Aldermen demanded that the Cumberland negotiate a new franchise with it for the privilege of operating in Louisville. The Board claimed that since the Ohio Valley Company had changed hands so often since 1886 its old franchise was no longer valid. The Cumberland replied that it had bought the franchise when it had bought the telephone poles. It took the dispute to the U.S. Supreme Court, which ruled that a city couldn't cancel a state contract. That left Louisville with only the right to quibble about rates. It also reminded the company that the best way to deal with politicians was to buy them.

Once the Cumberland had won its fight in the Supreme Court, the local investors who owned the Home Telephone in Louisville decided that it was only a matter of time before the Cumberland came knocking at their door, money in hand, ready to buy them out. They did what they could to speed the day. In 1916, a vice president of the Home Telephone Company, who had once been a Kentucky appeals court judge, talked the state legislature into repealing an 1891 Populist constitutional amendment which had forbidden telephone monopolies. The judge told the legislators that the house of Morgan was only waiting for them to change the law so that it could order its Cumberland Company to snatch up the Home. They had to wait six years for that to happen. In the meantime, the Cumberland had acquired more than nine million customers and 400,000 telephones in Illinois, Kentucky, Tennessee, Mississippi, and Louisiana.[8]

In 1921, the Cumberland began negotiations with the Home by renting Chelsey Searcy and John Doolan, his Democratic counterpart, for $10,000 a year. It hired them to act as counsels to get a rate increase from the city. A month before the 1921 election, the president of the Board of Aldermen claimed to have seen Searcy and Doolan walking out of the office of Mayor Smith accompanied by Cumberland officials. Searcy confessed he was on retainer, but he said he saw nothing wrong with it. The president of the Board, who was a Democrat, denounced him for taking money while he was chairman of the Sinking Fund. A Democratic paper wrote an editorial on the subject, and then nothing more was heard of it.[9]

The Cumberland paid Searcy not just because it could afford to, and Searcy took the money and confessed not just because he was shameless. The Cumberland paid, Searcy collected, and no one made a fuss because some of the most proper and wealthy gentlemen in the city presided over the sale of the Home like judges at an inquest. There were three in particular. One of them was J. B. Brown, another was J. W. Barr, and the third was W. R. Cole. Cole and Barr were both directors of the Cumberland and Brown was director of the Home.[10] Barr and Brown both lived in Louisville; Cole lived in Nashville but participated in the executive operation of the Louisville & Nashville Railroad. Once the money had changed hands and the rates had gone up, Barr lost interest in telephones, but Brown had himself appointed to the Cumberland board,[11] and soon after, he and Cole were both named directors of South Central Bell. All three of the men did many things other than direct the sale of a local company to a regional one.

Cole and Barr had almost interchangeable biographies. They both occupied genteel positions and exploited traditional investment opportunities. Whitefoord Cole's father had been president, for thirty years, of the East Tennessee, Virginia, and Georgia Railroad. Cole had been president of the Nashville, Chattanooga, & St. Louis Railway, a division of the Louisville & Nashville, since 1918. He had been an intimate friend of the L & N's president, and had succeeded him on his death in 1926. When he wasn't running a railroad, he sat in quiet rooms where a dozen or so men discussed what to do next with their money. Cole sat on the boards of the American National Bank of Nashville, the Nashville Trust Company, the Napier Iron Works, the Crescent Coal Company, and the American Cyanimid Company. He was also president of the board of trustees of Vanderbilt University, Chelsey Searcy's alma mater.[12] His colleague, J. W. Barr, also directed banks and universities. He had been a trustee at Princeton when Wood-

row Wilson was its president, and had been largely responsible for the government's decision to build Camp Knox and Camp Taylor close to Louisville during the First War. He was a director of the Fidelity-Columbia Trust Company, and he sat on the board of the Louisville Gas & Electric Company, and of the Louisville Cement Company, owned by the Speed family. Both Cole and Barr were restless men. Cole commuted so often by train between Nashville and Louisville that he died in his private car somewhere in-between. Barr was the sort who traveled several times to Europe, only to return a few days later with the explanation that the ocean voyage was the thing he enjoyed the most.[13]

Jim Brown was just as restless, but he never went to college. He made himself. He was born in 1872 in Lawrenceburg, Kentucky. He came to Louisville when he was seventeen. John Wallen, the old Democratic boss who ran a burlesque theater and did his best, along with August Belmont and the Louisville & Nashville Railroad, to keep the Populists out of the statehouse, gave Brown his first job as a cashier in the city's Tax Receiver's office. By 1901, Brown had been elected to the job. He had begun.

He learned who had what, and how much. The First National Bank hired him as a cashier. He watched the money move from one place to the other. By 1906, he was president of the bank. He became interested in what were called "mergers." At a distance, these resembled smaller fishes being eaten by bigger ones. Close up, each was seen to swim with a smile into the other's grinning mouth. Brown watched as the federal government broke up Standard Oil. Dozens of state and regional oil companies and hundreds of local ones grew from the pieces. He bought stock in Standard Oil of Kentucky and counted the dividends as that corporation bought out the speculators who had opened up the oil fields in the central and southwestern parts of the state. In 1907, Robert Bingham, who was Democratic mayor for that year, made him president of the Sinking Fund. He kept that job for eleven years until Chelsey Searcy took it from him after the First War.

In 1908, he tried his first merger: he had himself appointed president of the Liquor License Board at the same time he was president of a realty company that owned dozens of corner bars, and was itself owned by a brewery. He practiced looking at the horizon while he took money from someone else's pocket and put it in his own. That was what was known as an "informal merger." He didn't try anything like that again until 1925. By then he was able to arrange a loan of $6 million to the Louisville Railway Company, on the condition that the company repay its bonds by purchasing all the electricity for its trolleys from the Louisville Gas and Electric Company whose director and vice president he had become.

In 1909, he was elected president of the National Bank of Commerce. It took him ten years to merge that bank with the National Bank of Kentucky and the American Southern National Bank. It took another nine years to control the stock of the Louisville Trust Company and the National Bank and Trust Company. By 1927, his National Bank of Kentucky was worth $170 million. It was the biggest bank in the South.

In 1919, between mergers, he organized and, with Robert Bingham, directed the Kentucky Jockey Club, which ran Churchill Downs and other Kentucky tracks until 1928, when it was taken over by a holding company called the American Turf Association, with which he was also connected. By 1923, the Jockey Club employed thirty state legislators. A year later,

Brown and Bingham parted company; Brown had decided to go into the newspaper business. He bought the *Herald* from the Schaffers of Chicago and the *Post* from the Knotts of Louisville, and merged them to compete with Bingham's morning *Courier* and his evening *Times*.

In 1925, the board of directors of the Louisville & Nashville Railroad met in New York to fill the empty seat left by August Belmont's son, August Belmont, who had died the year before. They were pleased to appoint Mr. Brown, who they believed to be a man of equal stature.

By December 1930, Mr. Brown had filed for bankruptcy. He sat through a few trials for fraud and embezzlement. It was hard to prove very much since he'd always conducted his business at night, very quietly, without an office or a secretary, over the telephone. He confessed that he'd spent $60,000 on some parties and a little gambling up in French Lick; otherwise he said very little. Bellboys at the Seelbach Hotel said he liked to watch the revolving doors, especially empty ones; he'd tip them just to keep them spinning.[14]

Mr. Brown, Mr. Barr, Mr. Cole, and Mr. Searcy had an influence on Mayor Huston Quinn. A little more than a year after he was elected, the Mayor announced that he had learned of plans for the sale of the Home Telephone Company to the Cumberland Telephone Company. He asked the General Council of the Board of Aldermen to approve a rate increase prior to the sale. He even asked them to give tacit approval to the sale itself, even though he knew and they knew that the Supreme Court and the ICC had long ago taken the responsibility from them. He pretended to try to convince them. He argued for the sale and the rate change in such a contradictory way that he sounded like Siamese twins having an argument.

He claimed that the merger itself would create an efficient monopoly, free from competition and duplication of the facilities; then he explained that "the greater the number of telephone stations in a system, the greater the cost of rendering the service per station."[15] He never explained how an expanded system could be more efficient if it cost more to operate. Nor did anyone remind him that the Cumberland charged its 18,000 customers an average of $1.20 more than the Home charged its 21,000 subscribers.

Several months later, every member of the Board of Aldermen, except the president, voted for the rate increase, and two months after that, the Louisville Trust Company made the Mayor a vice president.[16]

Peter Coravitous was a Greek who had lived in Louisville for eleven years. He ran a restaurant, lived alone in a boardinghouse, and had $10,000 saved in the bank. One day when he went to the post office, he met a man who asked him for directions. A few days later, he met the man again. The man was so glad to see him that he introduced him to his uncle, Mr. DeFough. Mr. DeFough told Peter that he'd found $45,000 in a post office transfer wagon. He said he had plenty of money himself, and wanted to leave what he'd found to the poor. The only trouble was that he was so sick that he had to leave right away for South America. He wanted to do good before he died, but he needed someone he could trust to give the money away. Each time Mr. DeFough met Peter, he wept and went on about how sorry he was for the poor and how much he needed a good man to rely on. When Peter offered to help, Mr. DeFough and his nephew asked him to prove himself. They told him that if he was sincere, he would trust them to hold some of his money while he gave away theirs. Peter went to the bank and drew out all his savings. Mr. DeFough put them in one box, and his nephew handed Peter another with the poor people's money in it. When Peter asked to see the money, Mr. DeFough hit him with a blackjack and his nephew chased him away with a gun.[18]

Josephine Traub answered an advertisement for a nurse. Instead of meeting a patient, she met Madame Dinler, the world-famous phrenologist. Madame Dinler told Josephine she could help her be healthy, wealthy, and wise. First, she told Josephine she had money. Josephine was surprised. She asked her how she knew she had $1,100 in the bank. Madame smiled but did not answer. Instead, she told Josephine that she was in love. Josephine was even more surprised. Then she told Josephine the name of the man. Josephine was overcome. It was then that Madame Dinler told her that she was in danger: the money that she had in the bank had been coined under an evil star and bore a curse. What was worse was that an unknown relative had just died in a foreign land and left her $100,000 which was under the influence of a malignant planet. Madame said she could help. If Josephine gave her $1,000, she would turn it into gold and carry it to the evil planet that ruled her new inheritance. The $1,000 in gold would outweigh the $100,000 in cash. One influence would cancel the other. Josephine would be free from the double curse, and $100,000 richer. All Josephine had to do was to give Madame Dinler the money. Josephine did. Madame Dinler said her journey would take ten days. When she didn't return, Josephine went to the police. She told them she was afraid that something had happened to the sweet old lady somewhere out in space.[19]

Fred Grimes: "Saturday night on Pearl Street about eight-thirty I was robbed. I went in a place where there was a lot of colored people and I was dancing with one girl and she took my pocketbook that had a twenty-dollar bill and a receipt for twenty-five in it. I identify that woman there, the defendant, as the one that robbed me. I didn't tell anybody the woman that robbed me had two fingers off her hand."[19]

"Mrs. Robert T. Walker states that 'on Friday the defendant Tippy Artful came to my house, I did not know him, he is a colored boy, I had a cottage for sale on Berkenmeyer avenue, and he claimed he wanted to look at the house with the intention of buying it, he and I went over to the house, after we had inspected the house, we stopped at the corner of Payne and Berkenmeyer and he said to me "did you see that man pick that purse up," and I said, "Yes, he picked up something." and the man who picked it up came on up to us and said; "did you see anything of a white poddle dog?" he claimed to be looking for a dog, then Artful said; "Young man when you find anything like that always go the other way.", and the man that picked up the pocket book said; "Since you have been kind enough to warn me I will divide with you and this lady." and all three of us walked together to Cavewood avenue and stopped; he handed the purse over to Tippy Artful, Artful looked in it and said there was Twenty One Hundred Dollars in there and a Hundred Dollar Liberty Bond.
" 'Finch and Artful said how much money can you let me have to change one of the five hundred dollar bills, and I told them I didn't have any money around the house except a Liberty of the value of fifty dollars and eight dollars in money, and they said can you get any more by tomorrow and I said I guess I could, so they came back to my house Saturday, I had already given them the Liberty Bond and my money on the day before and when they came back Saturday I told them I wanted the Liberty Bond and my money back; Artful was by himself on Saturday morning, and when I asked him for my bond and money back, he said I will give it to you and he and I went out of the house and he told me to wait on the corner and he made his getaway.' "[20]

———————————

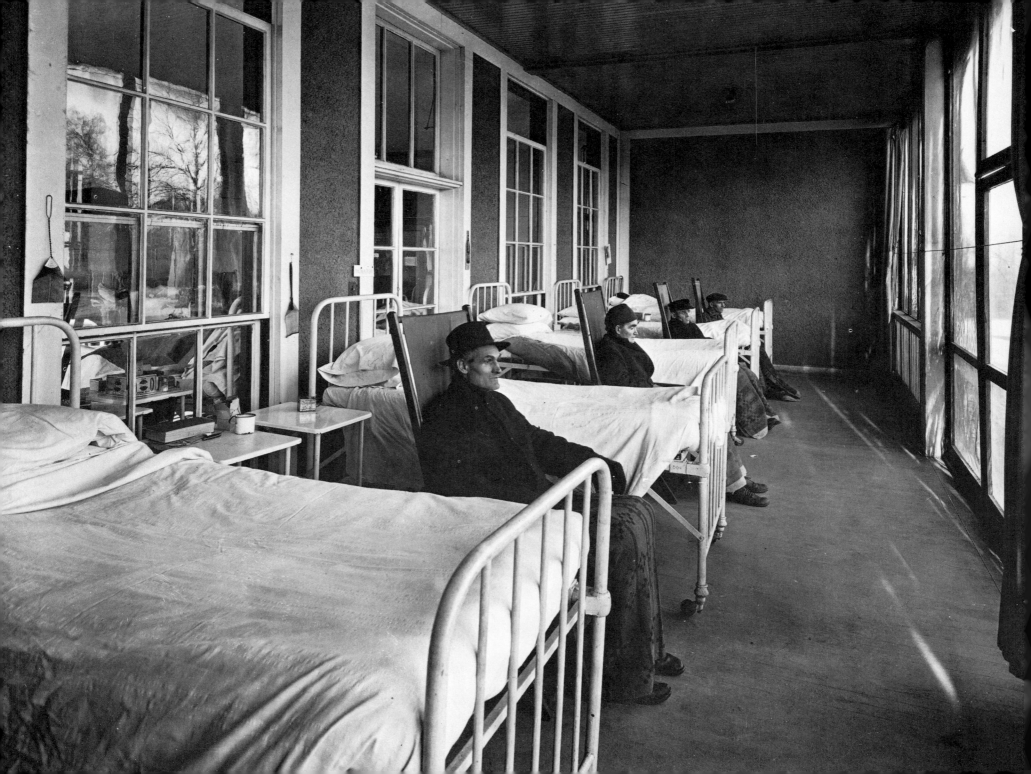

Brown and Searcy and Barr and Cole were not very different from either very young children or very deluded madmen, all of whom occasionally believe the world to be a mirror whose reflected objects can be changed as quickly as a thought. The only difference was that such men as Brown and Searcy had more patience than children, and that the objects they manipulated had more substance than the fantasies of lunatics. It was only because they believed so deeply in appearances that they learned to create illusions. They learned how to make passive men, overcome with their own appetites, appear to be disinterested and autonomous. They learned how to make events that were nothing more than points of reference on a map appear to be features of a natural landscape. Because they lived deeply within the plans of their minds, they were able to create plausible worlds to satisfy the expectations of others.

There were two dangers to such activities. One, the obvious one, was failure from discovery by others. The other was success. That was a danger because every event they created became more imaginary and less able to sustain itself without the attention they had already turned to something even less plausible. The telephone merger and the municipal election were nothing more than exercises in the witty juxtaposition of disparate elements to create an unlikely end. Brown and Barr learned that they could make a mountain out of a mole hill without anyone in the audience asking for their money back. Once they learned that, they tried something else. They tried to make something out of nothing.

The nothing in this case was the Kentucky Wagon Manufacturing Company. It had begun the decade worth $1.4 million but ended it owing $2.78 million to Jim Brown's bank. The president of the company was R. V. Board, a man who came to Louisville in 1913 from Boston, where he had directed the New England division of International Harvester. He arrived just in time to help J. W. Barr help the government to fight the war. Louisville got Camp Taylor and Camp Knox, and Mr. Board became a dollar-a-year man who coordinated the government's purchase of horse-drawn vehicles.[21] Every wagon his factory made went to France. In the course of the war, Mr. Board acquired a partner named James Duffin. They performed together until 1929, slowly perfecting a trick which made sums of money appear and disappear into thin air. Duffin's earliest experience with numbers had been as a mathematics teacher in Indiana. He then served as a county school superintendent for four years. Each year he built a new high school. In 1903, he came to Louisville to practice law as a junior partner in the firm of a Harvard man who became a Republican governor in 1907. By the time he met Mr. Board, he had become president of the InterSouthern Life Insurance Company. He had built his own company headquarters without a contractor by hiring his workers day by day.[22]

Duffin and Board performed together for the first time in 1920. Board had become one of the managing directors of a local oil company and Duffin, as his counsel, had sold the company to Atlantic Refining of Philadelphia for $5.4 million worth of stock in Superior Oil — a company owned by Atlantic. There were three conditions to the sale: Duffin, Board, and two of his partners were free to cash $2.9 million worth of the Superior stock immediately, but they had to wait until 1922 to cash the rest, and they had to pay all the federal taxes on the transaction.[23] Exactly two years after the sale, a dozen Louis-ville shareholders sued them all. They claimed that they had been paid only eighty cents on every dollar owed them from the $2.9 million that Duffin, Board, and his partners had acquired in 1920, and they demanded to know what had become of their share of the $2.5 million worth of stocks that were to have been sold in 1922. The only explanation that Duffin gave was that he was still arguing with the federal government over how much tax was owed on the original transaction. He never explained what he and Board and one of the other men had done with $900,000 of the money they had been paid in 1920.

One year after Board and Duffin had sold the local oil company, and one year before they were sued for performing magic in public, they began to look around for someone to buy the Kentucky Wagon Company. The Wagon Company had done so well during the war that the French had given Mr. Board a gold watch.[24] The company had continued to do well until 1921, when the wholesale commodity index fell from 226.7 to 143.3.[25] That price drop ruined the cotton farmers in Alabama, Georgia, and Mississippi who had been Kentucky Wagon's primary customers. When suppliers started to send bills that Mr. Board couldn't pay, he borrowed $250,000 from the banks, and wrote notes for another $750,000. Those loans and notes bought Mr. Board and Mr. Duffin seven months, during which they convinced an automobile and a truck company and three auto parts manufacturers to merge with Kentucky Wagon and form a new company called Associated Motor Industries. John W. Barr of Fidelity-Columbia Trust did what he could by filing papers of incorporation for Associated

Motor in Delaware. In January 1922, Board and Duffin announced that Kentucky Wagon was about to be purchased by a $40 million automobile and truck company, whose plants in six states would employ 5,000 workers to manufacture 10,000 four- and six-cylinder "pleasure cars" a year.[26]

The only trouble was that no one knew if petitions of receivership for Kentucky Wagon would clear the federal district court before the merger was completed. Two months after Board's announcement, shareholders of Kentucky Wagon had filed petitions of involuntary bankruptcy naming Duffin, Board, and Barr as defendants. The petitions claimed that Board was an incompetent who was trying to ruin the widows and orphans who owned $400,000 of the company's stock. The petitions also claimed that Kentucky Wagon owed $2.5 million to its creditors and that half of the companies named as divisions of Associated Motor were already bankrupt.[27]

Board coughed, cleared his throat, and waited three months to take another breath. Then he admitted that he'd been wrong. He said that Associated Motors was actually worth $50 million—$10 million more than he'd thought. Besides that, he said, the majority of Kentucky Wagon's shareholders and creditors were so pleased with the proposed merger that the papers would be signed in a week.[28] Duffin supported him by trying to convince the federal district court to delay its bankruptcy proceedings until the end of June. He confessed that Associated Motor was worth only $20 million. The court agreed to allow Kentucky Wagon to write a new set of notes that would fall due the next year.[29]

While Duffin and Board stood pointing in different directions with their eyes crossed, the papers were signed.

That same month, the Union Trust Company of Chicago advertised the sale of $6 million worth of ten-year gold bonds, bearing 7.5 percent interest, issued by Associated Motor Industries. The bank's ad listed Kentucky Wagon, the National Motor Car Company of Indianapolis, The Traffic Truck Company of St. Louis, The Recording and Computing Company of Dayton, a transmission company from New York, and a sheet metal company from Michigan as Associated Motor divisions. In July, the former president of Dayton Recording and Computing, now chairman of the Associated board, visited Louisville to make some important announcements. He said that contrary to what others may have claimed, Associated Motor was really worth $80 million. He said the company would employ 3,500 people in Louisville and 20,000 throughout the country. There were plans to link the company's plants in Boston, Indianapolis, St. Louis, and Oakland by radio. He said, "We will start production at full speed. Prosperity is here now . . . The policy of the corporation is against wage reduction and at the same time favors price reduction."[30] No one ever heard of him again.

In February 1923, the Jefferson County sheriff sold whatever lumber he could find in the Kentucky Wagon plant to satisfy a $68,000 debt. Duffin said the company could have paid the bill, but that "it was not within the properties of the situation."[31] He promised his creditors that every penny the company owed them would be paid by December, when the National Motor Car Company of Indianapolis was to purchase Kentucky Wagon and all its problems. The chairman of the board of Lincoln Bank and Trust Company, a trustee of the banks which by then held $1 million of the company's bad

paper, assured Mr. Duffin that everyone sympathized with him.[32] Neither the bank's sympathies nor Mr. Duffin's sense of propriety kept the Wagon Company's other creditors from demanding payment. A rubber company from Massachusetts advertised the sale of Kentucky Wagon to satisfy a $40,000 debt; the first group of creditors, who had been put off by the federal court in 1922, returned in July with their notes still unpaid, and a third group, whose claims totaled less than $1,200, filed a petition of their own. The banks, which by then had too much to lose, persuaded the federal judge to temporarily prevent the auction arranged by the rubber company.[33] The judge agreed to this because he'd been told that Jim Brown and J. W. Barr had arranged a meeting with the president of the National Motor Company—the new name given Associated Motor after the National Motor Car Company of Indianapolis had agreed to pick up the pieces.[34] There are no records of the meeting, but from the announcements made afterward and the arrangements and accusations that lasted until 1931, some inferences can be made: While Board and Duffin sat and listened, Brown explained that his National Bank had bought a major portion of the $2.78 million worth of notes that the Wagon Company had left behind. He and Barr, who had helped Board and Duffin arrange the original merger with Associated when Kentucky Wagon was between $1 million and $2.5 million in the hole, invited the president of National Motor to make them a reasonable offer. It took them four hours to decide how much the corpse was worth. Brown finally agreed to return the body for the $5 million worth of gold bonds that Union Trust Company of Chicago had advertised for sale in June of 1922. The president of National Motor was so relieved that he threw in the Wagon Company's mortgage and told Brown he could bury it himself. Brown did. He paid off the small creditors either with a few of National Motor's gold bonds, or with new notes signed by Kentucky Wagon, or with twenty-five cents, cash-on-the-line, for every dollar Kentucky Wagon owed them. He then sent Mr. Board and Mr. Duffin out to the factor to make some wagons.[35] Five months later, Mr. Duffin expressed his gratitude by having Mr. Brown elected chairman of the board of InterSouthern Life. One of the first things Mr. Brown did was to retire Mr. Duffin and then sell the company to some associates in Nashville.[36]

Kentucky Wagon lasted until Mr. Brown went bankrupt in 1930. Until then, the company stumbled, once a month and every month, to the National Bank of Kentucky where it paid $14,000 interest on the debt it owed Mr. Brown. One of Kentucky Wagon's vice presidents, a man named Gigax, said that trying to run the company under those circumstances was like trying to make a Ford go forty miles an hour with a ton of pig iron tied to the end of it.[37]

Notes

1. Anonymous Interview, September 23, 1975.
2. Louisville *Herald*, September 21, 1923, front page; Louisville *Courier-Journal*, September 21, 1923, front page.
3. *Courier-Journal*, May 10–12, 1935, December 1, 1938; *Who's Who in Louisville* (Louisville, Ky.: Standard Printing Co., 1926).
4. Louisville *Times*, October 1–8, 1921.
5. *Times*, October 18–25, 1921.
6. *Times*, November 3, 1921.
7. *Times*, November 7, 1921.
8. *Moody's Public Utilities and Industrials* (New York, 1919).
9. *Louisville Civic Journal*, October 8, 1921; *Times*, October 8, 1921.
10. *Moody's*; *Herald Post*, March 9, 1926.
11. *Courier-Journal*, July 4, 1926.
12. *Herald Post*, March 9, 1926.
13. *Times*, May 4, 1941.
14. *Courier-Journal*, October 25, 1940; *Times*, October 25, 1940; *Harpers Monthly*, September 1937, pp. 400–421.
15. *Herald*, February 6, 1924.
16. *Herald*, November 11, 1924.
17. *Herald*, August 4, 1924.
18. *Herald*, March 29, 1923.
19. Jefferson County Criminal Court, Case #48892, 1923.
20. Criminal Case #45116, 1921.
21. *Courier-Journal*, January 3, 1948.
22. *Who's Who in Kentucky* (Louisville, Ky.: Standard Printing Co., 1936).
23. *Courier-Journal*, August 8, 1920.
24. *Courier-Journal*, January 3, 1948.
25. U.S. Bureau of Labor Statistics, *Statistical Abstracts of the United States*, 1925.
26. *Courier-Journal*, January 22, 1922.
27. *Courier-Journal*, March 28, 1922.
28. *Courier-Journal*, June 11, 1922.
29. *Courier-Journal*, July 8, 1923.
30. *Courier-Journal*, January 7, 1922.
31. *Courier-Journal*, February 14, 1923.
32. *Ibid.*
33. *Courier-Journal*, July 8, August 9, 1923.
34. *Courier-Journal*, August 9, 1923.
35. *Louisville Post*, April 29, 1924; *Herald*, May 9, 1924, September 17, 1924.
36. *Courier-Journal*, February 10, 1925; March 17, 1938.
37. *Courier-Journal*, February 12, 1931.

Whites

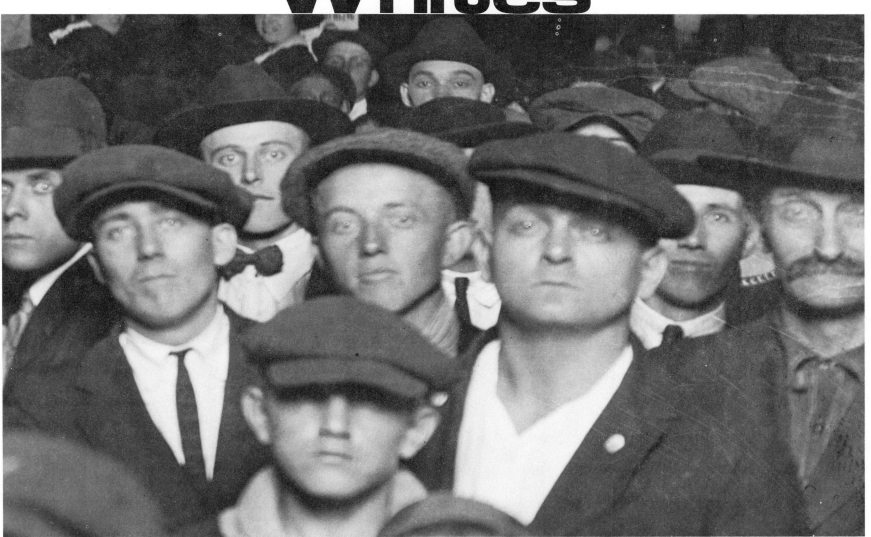

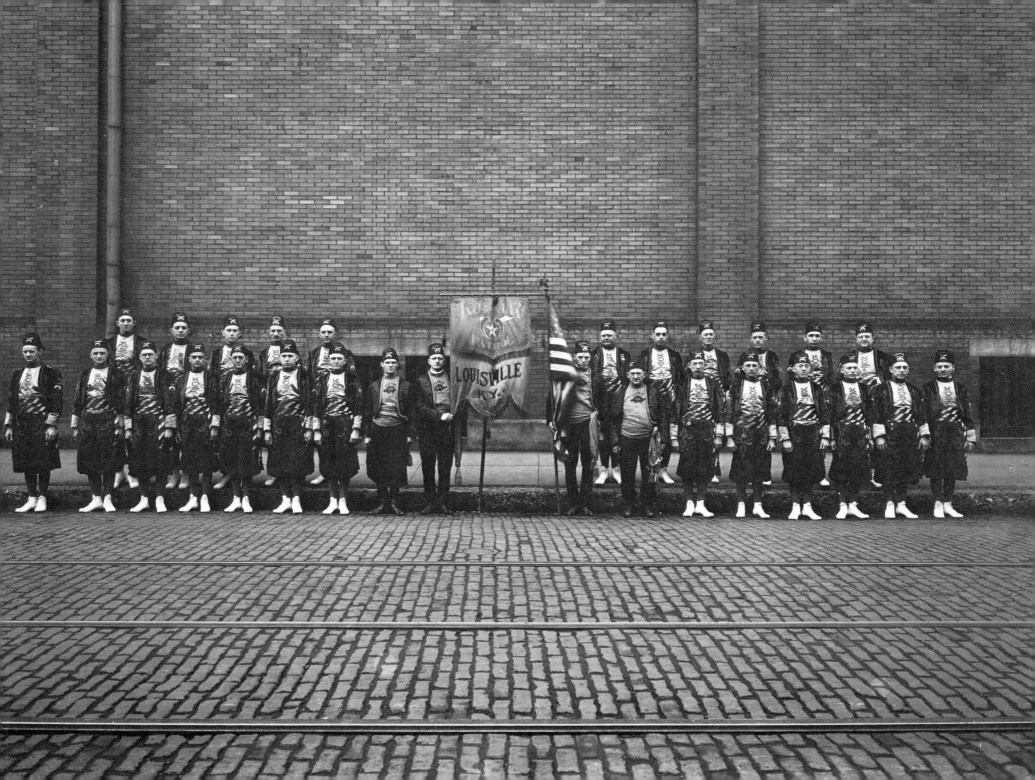

Caron's City Directory estimated the total population of the city of Louisville in 1924 to be 310,788. The U.S. Bureau of Census believed it to be 293,440. Eighty percent of the people were native-born whites.[1] They died of either cancer or pneumonia.[2] In 1924, which was the healthiest year of the decade, the white birth rate per 1,000 was 21.9.[3] In that same year, the death rate per 1,000 was 12. For comparison, in 1921, the birth and death rates had been, respectively, 17 and 12.8.[4]

On October 21, 1923, the Herald reported that the city's businesses paid an average wage of $1,057 per year to 59,000 workers, of whom 13,000 were women. This report was derived from figures published by Caron's. A U.S. Department of Commerce report (issued in 1929) estimated that in 1923, there were 715 factories and businesses in the city; that 37,620 people worked in them; and that they earned an average wage of $1,121 per year. A 1933 statistical abstract prepared by a group of Louisville sociologists analyzed the employment records of thirty-seven major firms that had been in the city since 1924.[5] It concluded that the average wage had been $1,355 per year in 1924. Whether the city's average wage in 1923–1924 had been $1,057 or $1,121 or $1,355, it was still below the 1923 national average of $1,383 calculated by the Department of Commerce.

Two weeks before the Herald published the city's employment figures for 1923, the Louisville & Nashville Railroad laid off 500 of the 3,500 men it employed in its locomotive and repair shops in the city. The railroad said that the 500 men had been hired to make up for lost time caused by the nationwide rail strike of 400,000 shopcraft workers that had begun in May 1922. That had been the largest rail strike in the country's history to that time; it had involved 15,000 men in Kentucky and had reduced the Louisville force to 1,000 union and non-union men. The strike had been called when wages were cut from sixty to fifty-five cents per hour—a cut that workers had testified would put them in the poorhouse. The railroads had already cut the wages of two million men by 12 percent, a year before, during the depression of 1921. The rail strike in Kentucky came at the same time as a coal strike in which 10,000 eastern Kentucky miners were opposed by National Guard troops armed with machine guns and tanks. The effect of these two strikes in Kentucky was to slowly stop coal from reaching the factories of the Midwest. Within three months, Henry Ford was pleading with the Louisville & Nashville to let him run his own trains, with his own crews, into and out of eastern Kentucky, where hundreds of coal cars were caught in the switching yards. Within four months, the Department of Justice had broken the strike with a federal injunction.[6]

In June 1924, the Louisville & Nashville once again laid off more men from its Louisville repair shops. The Herald attributed the layoffs to a business slowdown that had caused the city's lumber, textile, and flour mills and meatpackers to operate only part-time.[7] In spite of this, there were still jobs to be had completing $13 million worth of nonresidential construction projects. These included a $3.5 million seminary; a $2 million municipal gas plant and a $2 million hardware warehouse; and an Elks Club and a Korsair Temple worth $2.75 million.

———————————————

The KKK held its first meeting in Louisville, in a park, one night in February 1923. Police were told about it after it had begun. When they got there, all they found was a half-burnt flagpole, some misspelled circulars, and the footprints of ten men. The circulars instructed the Klansmen to sell ten new memberships in ten days, and to keep their mouths shut and their ears open. The next day, the Mayor and the Chief of Police called them a dumb bunch of chicken thieves. Two weeks later, the Klan burnt a cross a half of a block from the Mayor's house. It was seventeen feet high, covered with cotton soaked in coal oil. In front of it was the skull of a black man, stuck on a wagon spoke, planted in the ground. The top of the skull had been sawed off, and there was only one tooth still in its jaws.

In June, some attorneys who said they represented the Klan asked to have a meeting with the Mayor and the Chief of Police at City Hall. They came in the front and left by the back. The Mayor told them the city wouldn't stand for any lawless demonstrations. They told him he had nothing to worry about. A few days later, the Reverend Mr. Parkes, pastor of the Portland Avenue Baptist Church, announced that he would sponsor a meeting to discuss and explain the principles of the KKK. The Mayor and the Chief of Police asked him to pay them a visit. After they had a little talk, Mr. Parkes canceled the meeting. On the Fourth of July, eighty-five Klansmen from across the river in Jeffersonville, Indiana, lit a cross on Third Street in the middle of Louisville. By the time the police arrived, they'd boarded a charter train for a Klan rally in Kokomo.

The Reverend Mr. Parkes tried to hold another meeting in his church at the end of September. He announced that the Reverend E. L. Lougher, a national organizer for the KKK, would speak about the organization's principles. This time the Mayor and the Chief of Police sent Mr. Parkes a letter. Only this time, even though Mr. Parkes said he'd cancel the meeting, a Klansman telephoned the newspapers to announce that Reverend Lougher would speak in a vacant lot next to the Cadle Tabernacle on Walnut Street that same evening. The police got there a little late. They opened a box of tear gas bombs and connected a firehose to a hydrant. They circled the block, stopped all traffic, and dispersed the 1,500 people who had come to see what would happen. Then they arrested the Reverend Mr. Lougher and charged him with inciting revolution, anarchy, and riot. They also arrested the Reverend Mr. Parkes when he tried to cross their line on Walnut Street. He pledged he'd preach a sermon on Sunday against the Mayor and the Board of Public Safety to "tear the mask from them in their efforts to destroy freedom of speech and assembly . . ."

The Reverend Mr. Bulgin, who had been conducting the revival at the Cadle Tabernacle, almost started a riot when he tried to walk through the police line carrying a big cross outlined in red light bulbs. The police let him through, but escorted him into the church. The Reverend Mr. Settle, the pastor of the Tabernacle, began the service by trying to introduce the Reverend Mr. Lougher, who'd already been arrested. He told the congregation that Mr. Lougher was a man "who has been denied the right of free speech on property that has been allotted to him." Then Mr. Bulgin got up and told them to turn off the lights. Everyone stared at the big red cross while Harry Box sang "When to the Cross I Turn." After the lights went back on, Mr. Bulgin began to speak. He said he wanted all the Masons to come to church on Sunday so that he could ask them about their vows. The audience said yes. He said he wanted all the Knights of Columbus there. The audience said yes. He said he wanted every Klansman there. The audience said yes, yes, and shouted. After it was quiet, he spoke to them on the subject of evolution. He wanted to know why the scientists couldn't make another Jesus or another Napoleon since they thought they were as good as God. Fourteen people came up to be saved.[8]

The rally on Walnut Street was the last anyone heard of the KKK in Louisville for almost a year. Then in June 1924, the Reverend Mr. Parkes made a confession to his congregation. He told them he'd been a Klansman, but he'd left it all behind. He said he'd learned that every member of the police court, except the judge, was a member of the KKK. He said the only thing they were interested in was spreading hate and selling ten-dollar memberships. A day later, the Reverend Mr. Lougher, who had been living in Lexington, tried to hold another rally in another vacant lot in Louisville. Another crowd of 1,500 came to listen. The police came and told him to stop. He kept on talking for another half-hour, until he got into an argument about religion. That's when the police arrested him. They said they were afraid a fight was going to start between half of the audience that was for him and half of the audience that was against him.[9]

98

"I was a water boy during the summer of '24 when

they built the Ford plant . . . I was fifteen. I had two buckets of water. One bucket was for the colored; one bucket was for the white people . . . There was a white band around the white one and a black band around the black one . . . I'd go along and set the bucket for the whites here and the other bucket for the colored on the other side. I got twenty-five cents an hour, which was big wages . . . I lent money on a percentage when I was carrying water. I made quite a few dollars on the men on the job—some of 'em would pay as high as twenty-five cents on the dollar to get money for the week. The going price would be about 10 percent. They'd want ten dollars to pay day, then they'd give you a dollar. That got around, 'cause I was water boy; the news got around fast—see, I contacted everybody on the job. I made quite a few dollars . . . I had my eyes open to make a buck . . . I never would smoke cigarettes because I wanted money in my pocket. I always had money in my pocket.

"I would go to the races and jump the fence and sell chairs and folding camp stools. We would buy 'em from someone— they would pass 'em under the fence to us for fifty cents apiece and we'd sell 'em for two dollars . . . I made as high as sixty dollars on Derby Day at the races. It was good money, couldn't make it doing anything else. We came home with our pockets full of money . . . I had the hustle and the bustle to make a dollar. I was determined to retire when I was thirty years old. But I didn't make it.

"April first, 1926, I was just eighteen years old. I went to work at the Ford plant. I told 'em I was twenty, that I'd worked for Studebaker and at Ford in Detroit . . . I was only too glad to get the five dollars a day, which was big money . . . I was on the closed-body trim line. I was there for three or four different models of cars—Model A's mostly.

"You had to be a hard worker to stay on at that Ford plant. There would be no loafing. Nothing but hard work . . . They were rough on you. If you just looked crooked, they'd fire you . . . You better not mention 'union' around that Ford plant. You didn't have a leg to stand on . . . At that time they would fire you if you bought another car other than their make. One fella I was working with, I was real close to, and he bought a Chrysler, a sixty-six, with a peep-peep horn, real classy and real good; bought a car and come in there the next day; he came in that parking lot with that Chrysler, and he went right out. They fired him that very same day. He didn't last two hours . . . If you had to go to the toilet, you had to get somebody to take your place. If he didn't hold up your part of the job, you'd get behind, and if you didn't get your work back up to where it belonged, they'd fire you for that . . . A lot of my buddies were from the country. You had to be good friends with your buddies for them to help you out. Everyone else was looking for your job. They'd line up outside the plant every evening for the night shift looking for work. They'd line up for years."[10]

Orville Stevens, alias Big Steve, alias the Deacon, was a Louisville car thief. He worked for Frank Hall, the Chief of the

Fayette County Police in Lexington. He stole Studebakers, and Frank bought them for fifty dollars apiece. Frank had a list of every Studebaker in Louisville and Lexington, and another list of all the Studebakers that belonged to people who were too important to be bothered. The Chief was a married man, but he was in love with Dorothy Tingle. Dorothy was the widow of a famous Cincinnati car thief who'd met the Deacon in jail. That's how Frank had hired him. Every time Dorothy wanted a new car, she got one, and every time the Deacon made a delivery, the Chief cleared every cop off the main road.

Orville stole nine cars in three months before they nailed him in Louisville. That's when he confessed. He said things hadn't begun very well. The first car he stole was a Studebaker Special Six from in front of the courthouse in Lexington. He didn't know it belonged to the former sheriff. But Frank did. He checked his list and told Orville he couldn't handle it. He said, "Drive it out on some road and leave it. You'll have to kick it back . . ." The second car went a little better, but not much. He lifted a Studebaker sedan from in front of some high-class apartments in Louisville, and delivered it to the Chief's assistant, Sargeant Barry. Barry didn't like it. He said it had initials on the doors. Then he said it was "a closed job that they couldn't use, but he would hold it and see what he could do with it . . ." The third car went worse. Orville was sitting in front of the same apartments as before when he saw a man who looked like a doctor get out of a Buick coupé and go up the elevator. It wasn't a Studebaker, but "I couldn't resist the temptation . . . After changing the tags which I grabbed off another car . . . I drove [it] to Lexington . . . I drove down to the colored section, called Chicago Bottoms, and left the car." He

knew the Chief wouldn't touch it because it wasn't a Studebaker. "I decided to sell it to a Negro that I heard in a roundabout way was O.K. . . ." The only trouble was that the Chief found out about Orville going into business for himself. He and the Sargeant beat the shit out of him, then drove him over to the city jail to have him arrested. Orville said he was sorry; the Chief let him wash the blood off his face, and then they dumped him on a train to Louisville. A brakeman found him in a heap on the back platform.

Orville said he'd confessed because the Chief had given him "a raw deal." A day later, Lexington police went looking for County Chief Hall. They found him behind the wheel of his Studebaker, with a bullet in his brain, a .38 Smith and Wesson beside him, and a suicide note written on the back of a blank check. Someone had torn it in half. It said, "I Fra . . ./Hall . . ./Estate . . ./Live . . ./a . . ." Frank's wife, Roxie, and his mother said he'd killed himself from grief, but the Deacon said "he didn't have the nerve . . . someone must have bumped him off . . . I thought he'd skip . . . and leave me and the other monkeys to face the music . . . We did the dirty work, but he copped the grapes." The police found a perfume bottle near the Chief's body. They went looking for Dorothy Tingle, but the last time anyone had seen her was when she got on the train for Detroit.[11]

12-24-25

10-30-7-5

"I did plumbing work and played saxophone on the

side . . . I went to work for Volks Brothers, July fifth, 1919 . . . and I stayed with that same firm all the way until the Depression . . . Playing music helped me learn the plumbing trade — see, I was just making six or seven dollars when I first started plumbing . . . then I picked up the music and that helped me out . . . I'd leave home at seven o'clock in the morning, get the streetcar, get to the job by seven-thirty, and start at eight. We'd work until four-thirty, then I'd come on home, clean up, get myself together, and go on downtown to play.

"We'd play soft music at a restaurant until seven thirty or we'd play at these theaters that had still pictures. We'd play until nine or nine-thirty; made three dollars a night. I used to have five different picture shows to play a week. I used to play the East Broadway twice a week, and down at Twenty-first and Portland, that's where I met my wife . . . We used to play dances everywhere in Louisville. We'd play club dances and dances down in a real rough place on F Street . . . We'd play stag parties the American Legion used to give. Dances were paying four-fifty and five dollars, and if you played to twelve o'clock, you was getting six dollars for it. I'd play in the pit at the Savoy Theater; they had Vaudeville. We used to play roadhouses. There was one roadhouse with a church next door. When that church would stop at nine o'clock, we'd start up, and it would go, Saturday night, to four or five o'clock Sunday morning. We played a public dance for two years every Saturday night, and we'd leave there, and sometimes the Law would be having a party at their house and we'd go there and play until three o'clock . . . Once in a while we used to go down to the center of town after we played dances and set in with some black musicians . . . some of the nicest places was up in these big mansions. They'd have parties after Derby Day, on a Sunday. Man, I tell you!

"Then I used to play with a traveling orchestra. They'd book us four or five engagements. We'd play at Centre College one night, then the next two nights would be in Nashville . . . We'd play at the Maxwell House, that was the main hotel down there. Then we'd drop down into Alabama or Mississippi. Then come on back up over into eastern Kentucky, at coal mining places . . . We went to play this place where they had the biggest coal tipple in the world. A real rough place. See, the Bethlehem Steel Company owned that town. It was really odd to see all these coal miners come out . . . dressed up . . . like a bunch of big apes . . . We had to stay in the hotel that night after the dance, and there was these two guys out in the hall, arguing about shooting one another. Boy, I tell you!

"It was a rough-ass job to travel. One time we were traveling from Nashville to Knoxville on a Sunday, and we decided to play some music to entertain the people on the train. So we was in the back coach and we got our instruments out and was playing and raising hell, and all the people from the whole damn train come back there and the conductor couldn't handle it no more, so he stopped the train and told us, 'You guys put your damn instruments away or we'll put you off the train!' . . . One night we played a dance up in Washington, Indiana, and they come up with a jug of whisky and put it down with four tin cups and said drink as much as you want . . .

"In Louisville, people brought their own booze. The biggest jobs would come off Derby Eve and New Year's Eve. At one club, they was serving whisky by the fifth. At two o'clock it was all over; people was going out the door, so I got myself a fifth and was going out the front door when some guy stopped us and asked us if we'd go down and play in a Pullman car the rest of the night at Tenth Street Station. They used to pull Pullman cars down there for the Derby. So we went down and played till daylight. Damn! Four or five drinks would be stacked up — you just couldn't keep up with 'em. One guy who played the tuba, he fell down the goddamn steps with the tuba around his neck. It was kind of a rough racket . . .

"One thing was that when I played, I refrained from drinking, because they always told me: "A whisky glass and a woman's ass will make a horse's ass out of you' . . . Women would come up and stuff like that, but I learned: Don't you fool with any of the women or you'll get yourself killed. Some of those roadhouses . . . some of 'em would get so plastered they wouldn't know what they was doing. I seen one time a guy drag a woman across the floor by *her hair* . . .

"I made more money playing music than plumbing . . . I bought three cars in six years. For five years, from '24 until '29, I didn't have a Saturday or Sunday night off. I'd be working as a plumber during the week . . . playing a picture show or a dance . . . but then, every Saturday and Sunday night, for five years steady."[12]

Bob Jones: "This fellow Jarbot came into my house and took me out of bed and took me down to the river at Shawnee Park and told me he was going to throw me in the river and make me swim if I didn't tell him where fifty cases of whiskey were. They said they were Revenue men and they wanted to know where that whiskey was and I told them I didn't know anything about it and they said I did and Jarbot hit me across the head while I was putting my shoes on sitting on the side of the bed and they put me in a machine and took me down to the river and said if I didn't tell them where it was they were going to run me in the river and make me swim or drown."

John Jarbot: "I live in Lexington, Kentucky. I have been living there for about eighteen years. On the night of the prize fight at the Jefferson Theatre I was in Louisville and after the prize fight I went to the Seelbach Hotel to call my mother and to tell I wouldn't come home and took my machine over on Sixth Street to have it fixed and while they were fixing it I went over to the Chief of Police office and talked to Captain Curran, that was about three or four o'clock in the morning, and waited there until the machine was fixed which was about five o'clock in the morning. I don't know Bob Jones I don't even know where his place is and I don't know anything about fifty cases of whiskey."[13]

"Most of the time he was drinking, so much that it interfered greatly with his work; so that he would lose his position if he had one and would have to accept odd jobs at carpentering . . . he was more interested in selling moonshine than in his regular work. I would often find the moonshine hid around different places in the house and on several occasions I threw it out, and he would quarrel with my daughter because it disappeared . . . On one occasion his brother, who also sold moonshine, was notified that the officers were on the trail, and two bags were brought to his coal shed . . . and hid there, and he told me that his brother Edgar had noticed that they were going to be raided and that they had hidden it there in his coal shed."[14]

The police walked up the steps of Joseph Steinberg's house just as he was pouring the last of a gallon of moonshine down his throat. They asked him what his hurry was. He said he'd heard his neighbors call them, so he'd decided to get it all inside before they came. "I was rowing up the river this afternoon and the jug came floating down."[15]

"One day I caught him in the yard with two drunken women, he had his arms around them, and they were all drunk. I got him and took him home, and he fought me on the way home, and told me those women were as good as I was. One day I came home and there was a woman sitting in my kitchen drinking whiskey with him. He was continually drunk. He was a vegetable peddler and as soon as he had finished his route he would get drunk. Often he was drunk on the wagon."[16]

"The first time he got drunk was four years ago, when he was a policeman, and they brought him home dead drunk in the machine, and put him on my bed, and he wasn't there five minutes until he got up and pulled out his gun, and started after me and ran me all over the streets with his gun in his hand and in his stocking feet and no shirt."[17]

L. T. Williams had a couple of drinks up in his room in Nora Bumper's boardinghouse. He came downstairs and said a few choice words to her. She told him not to use such language in front of the children. He went back up, got his gun, shot her in the belly, and then shot himself in the head. She lived; he died. The neighbors had a hard time comforting Mrs. Bumper's crippled son. Her daughter wouldn't leave the house until she'd found her prayer book.[18]

Bill Puckett, his brother Vernon, and a neighbor came home drunk at two o'clock in the morning. When Puckett's mother wouldn't let him in, he said he'd kill her and her new husband. He beat up his brother, tore a piece off the picket fence for a club, and smashed out a window. Bill's wife Mary grabbed their baby, and ran out front to try to stop him. That's when Bill's stepfather came to the front door and took a shot at him. The bullet missed Bill, but killed the baby.[19]

Thomas Crawley boarded with his brother Elijah and Elijah's wife. Elijah was twenty-eight and worked for the K & I Railroad; Thomas was forty and drank. He got nasty one day and beat up Elijah's wife. The next day, Elijah spotted him coming through the backyard. He shouted for him to get out. Thomas reached for his hip pocket to pull out his pint, but Elijah thought he'd gone for his gun. He shot him through the heart. Thomas fell on his back, and the whisky soaked through his pants, between his legs. "It was that devil, that . . . moonshine in him that I shot at."[20]

"There were more fine mechanics per square inch in Germantown than in any part of any city in the whole country. Across the street from us was the best and cleanest grocery you'd ever walk into. People from all over the neighborhood would come in. Had a big porch out front. In the morning, the women would stand around and talk . . . The old man who ran it—every Friday night, the old man would start to clean in there. The floors were scrubbed; the counters were scrubbed; twice a year he took all the canned goods off the shelf . . . and he scrubbed the shelves until he almost took the varnish off. Twice a year he washed the ceiling down. Anything you wanted, it was there. That old man was out at four o'clock in the morning; take his horse and wagon, go to the market, come back around seven, unload the stuff. His wife would open. His son was the butcher. That old man would go all day, never stop. It looked like the wind would blow him away anytime.

"Most of my relatives were plasterers. My dad and I were the only bricklayers. I started as an apprentice in 1913. I was only fifteen, but I lied about my age. We had to go four years to one contractor. When you were indentured to a man, you were more or less his slave, but he really taught you the business . . . We started out at fifty cents a day. When I finished in 1917, we were getting sixty-two and a half cents an hour . . . You took a streetcar to the job . . . you carried your tools *on your back*. It wasn't so easy for a fellow to get on a streetcar . . . with your four-foot level and a big bag of tools . . . When we went on the job in the morning, the boss stood there, and you were *on the scaffold* at eight o'clock. He stood there; you thought he had a stop watch. He'd say, 'Let's go,' and you went until twelve. You ate on the scaffold. At twelve-thirty, you were *on the scaffold* when he said, 'Let's go,' and you kept going until quitting time. There was no let-up, you just laid brick continually. You had to lay a couple thousand a day.

"It was just as hard for me working for my daddy as for any contractor, because he wouldn't let up. Half the time he'd never hear a whistle blow. You'd have to tell him it was twelve o'clock; but he always knew when it was time to go back to work . . . We didn't work on any of the big office buildings. Some of the contractors had cliques; they'd have four or five pets they'd always hire. Those guys got away with murder, but any stranger had a hard time making it. He'd have to do a lot more work than they did; they had the best spots on the wall; they raised the leads, and you got out there and beat your brains out on the line. . . We did residential work. My dad was a small contractor and that's what he got. We built all the big, beautiful homes. We built fine homes in places like Crescent Hill . . . You worked six months a year. October, work would dry up, and that was all until spring opened in March or April. What money you made didn't last very long. There wasn't anything you could save.

"When there wasn't any work after World War I, I decided to go into the police department for a while. I walked the Smoke Town Beat. Those black devils came back from France—some of 'em were tough. I only had trouble with one, the first day I was on. He was on a streetcar; he claimed some of the fellows were making fun of him. He started a row . . . I finally had to club him because he was tough. I brought him in, sent him to the workhouse for fifteen days, and never had any more trouble with him after that. Never had any trouble with any of those colored people . . .

"I got married in 1921. My wife was Irish . . . she was a waitress and one of the best. She'd carry more dishes! I didn't know how she did it. She worked at the best restaurants in town. I made up my mind on the spur of the moment. I never consulted my daddy about it. We weren't too close in matters of that type . . . Pop was sore about it. I didn't go to work for a couple days. Finally when I showed up, he wanted to know where the hell I'd been. I told him I'd got married, and he didn't speak to me for about a month until my wife and I decided to get remarried at the Cathedral one night. After that, everything seemed all right. We were never able to have any children . . . my wife had an operation and that finished that . . .

"When the Depression hit, I came home one night to borrow money from my dad to pay my rent. He said, 'I'll be paying your rent for years. This is a depression.' I said, 'Well, what am I gonna do?' He said, 'Get your rags and come on home.' So I did."[21]

———————————

When Albert Schaub was eighteen, he'd graduated from the best high school in the city, with honors in his studies, trophies for track and wrestling, and medals for ROTC drill. He went to work as a machinist for an elevator company, but after three years, he "was tired of being poor." He wanted to "be somebody." His father worked as a gardener for a man who'd grown rich making paint. The man lived in a house with servants, facing a beautiful park. One night in March, while the man's family and servants were at dinner, Albert stole $4,000 worth of jewelry and $300 in cash. The police caught him, but he returned nearly everything and the man forgave him.

Nine months later, he robbed a movie theater. The police arrested him again. He told the jury that he'd gotten another job as a toolmaker, but that he'd been laid off. "Other young

men will sometimes find themselves in my condition . . . For three or four weeks, I went to manufacturing and other places seeking work, but was always told that times were slack and that they were laying men off. I owed board bill . . . [I] contemplated suicide, but I couldn't get up my nerve . . . I was compelled to commit this robbery. I had nothing to eat, and no place to stay, so I did this. I paid the landlady the bill that I owed her. I do not know how much money I got . . . I didn't count it . . . The gun I used was not loaded . . . I had borrowed it . . . I had no money to buy cartridges. Rather than shoot a man, I would prefer to be shot myself. I had a mash on [a few drinks] when I did it." He got ten years.[22]

A. P. Mohrman (4117 W. Broadway): "He struck me with a pair of ice hooks yesterday morning about ten o'clock. He came down and I was in the wagon yard and he said to me: 'Mr. Mohrman, I have quit.' I said: 'Alright, take your hooks into the office and come back Saturday afternoon and get your money.' He said: 'Alright, sir.' He went into the office and the young lady said: 'This man wants his money.' I said: 'He has quit and he will come back Saturday afternoon for his money when we pay off.' He said: 'I am going to have my money now.' I said: 'You cannot get it now.' He said: 'Well fire me and give it to me.' I said: 'There is no use you have quit.' He said: 'You have to give it to me right now.' I said: 'I don't want to have any trouble with you, go on about your business.' The young lady said: 'You haven't left these hooks in here.' He said: 'No, I will give them to him over his head when he comes out.' I was not paying any attention, and when I went out with a bill of lading he smacked me across the face with those hooks and I jumped back and he struck at me and ran out into the street and came back, and I was in the wagon yard, and he said: 'I'm not through with you yet.' He struck at me a couple of times and I hit him and the officer got him in the street."/Q. "Did it stick you in the nose when he hit you?"/A. "When he hit me with the hooks it did that."[23]

"About 6 P.M. on the Fourth of July, i stopped my truck in the front of a friends house on Breckenridge Street between Fifteenth and Sixteenth Streets in the rear, after i was in the house i looked out and seen some boys tampering with my truck, i then went back out to the truck to put the tailgate up which they had dropped, and told them to let the truck alone, about that time a fellow who i did not know, stepped up and began cursing me. At this time the women who i was visiting whose name is Alma, came out to the truck and pulled me into the house, this man who was cursing me fired a pistol thru the front window, at me then i fired back at him thru the front window, i fired one time, then he run to the back of the house, thru the side yard, Then i came out to my truck and said to Emmett Daley, 'crank my truck and lets get away from here,' He cranked the truck and we started down the alley, i looked back and seen this man coming after me with an ax, in his hand, the spark was up on my truck and it would not run fast enough to get away from him, he run up to the side of the truck with the ax drawn over his head, i seen i could not get away from him so i said to the man with me, Emmett Daley, to take the truck, he took hold of the wheel and i stepped out on the running board of the truck and fired one shot at him then he fell, then i went to my Mother's home."[24]

"This will happen sometime in September or on this very afternoon. I have found where my wife is living and furthermore, that she is living with a man whose name I do not know. But that makes no difference, for I am going to kill them both as well as myself, if I can, and my troubles will then be over on this earth. It is on account of our children that I am doing this. And a mother that will treat her babies the way she has done ought to be killed and this will be a warning to others that are doing the same. Well, I have $750 in insurance that will put us away.

"Some people will say 'that man is insane', but that is not true. I have strived this over and begged her not to lead this kind of life, but she would not listen to me. So they that will not stop will have to take the punishment. You can send our bodies to Mr. John B. Turn at Sellersburg, Kentucky.

"The Bible says that man is born of woman but in a few days and full of trouble. That is my life. I love my dear children and I hope they will let my mother raise them and that she will be good to them. So let this be a warning to crooked women to do right and be true to their husbands.

"This is the finish of a wrecked life that a woman had made.

So good bye to all
(Signed) Robert Vern[25]

"The dying statement of the man who was killed read as follows:
Q. 'Tell us who shot you and what did he shoot you for? You want to tell everthing before you die don't you?'
A. 'Wait til I get my breath.
'Well my wife has been going with some man with a red face and tall wears a blue suit, I think they call him William or something, he is I think about forty years of age. I met my wife tonight at Twelfth and Broadway, did not expect her to be there, she came along while I was sitting on a bread box in front of the place or on the side. The grocery is on the northeast corner of Twelfth and Broadway. Well, I was talking to her when this big fellow came across the road and stopped at the curb, then walked up to my wife and said what are you doing with her, and I said what the hell do you care, and he said that ain't your wife, that's my girl. I don't know what the fellows name is, but when I grabbed hold of my wife's coat another man came up, I think he got off the street car, and separated me from the hold I had on her, this big man backed away and said to hell this is not your wife, if she is she will soon be mine, I backed away and the street car man shot and after I fell this big fellow plugged me and the other man run to a car on the corner. The big fellow drew his gun first and shot twice, and the street car man shot once. I don't know what became of my wife I dont know where she went to.' "[26]

"When we got over by the Racing Derby device we saw him and Ted Barber with two young girls; and they went on the Racing Derby about four times, and the defendant had his arm around the young lady all the time. We watched them there, and then they got off there and went over to the Canals of Venice, which is a device for a boat ride through the long and dark passages, and we got a boat right behind the one in which he and Ted Barber and the two girls were in, and almost near the end of the ride we got up real close to them, and . . . I heard him say to the girl he was with 'Whose little girl are you now?' and she said 'Nobody's' and then she said, 'I am my own sweet mama.' At the end of the ride they got off and went to Hilarity Hall."[27]

"On the night of September 20, 1924, at the meeting at the Gospel Home Mission, 1711 West Market Street, Mr. Numer got up and said that Brother Loughlin was no fit person to preach the gospel, and gave as his reason, that he, Loughlin, had been intimate with his wife and had broken up his home. Mrs. Numer was present at this meeting and heard what her husband had said, and after he sat down she got up and said that what her husband had said was true, that Mr. Loughlin had overpowered her and had been intimate with her, that he had been to her house as often as three or four times a day."[28]

". . . and this fellow Cross comes in there and puts his collar and necktie on the box in the room where my wife was in bed and that was the first time in my life that I ever knew his eyes were bad and he could not see to get out the door, he said he was pretty near blind and I went and asked my wife, I said, Darling why did Mr. Cross have to come in here this morning before eating his breakfast and she said well I will tell you the only thing I know he said he was highly delighted on account of belonging to the Masons and I said that is the first time I ever knew that talking about belonging to the Masons would put a man stone blind."[29]

"So, the day he left, it was around one o'clock in the day, and he had been sitting in the kitchen smoking a cigarette, and kinda mumbling to himself off and on, and so finally he got up and put his hat on, and started out and said to her that he was gone, and she asked him what was the matter, and he said he was tired of it all, 'he didn't like married life no how,' and went out, and he has never been back since."[30]

Notes

1. *Compilation of Basic Data, Economic and Social,* anonymous, unpublished manuscript, 1933 (Kentucky Room, Louisville Public Library).
2. *Ibid.*
3. *Ibid.,* based on the U.S. Bureau of Census.
4. *Report,* U.S. Bureau of Census, 1929, and *Annual Report, 1921,* Louisville Board of Health.
5. *Compilation of Basic Data.*
6. Louisville *Courier-Journal,* July 1 – October 1, 1922; H. E. Jones, *Wages and Labor Relations in the Railroad Industry, 1900 – 1941,* Information Bureau of the Eastern Railroads, 1941, pp. 73 – 79.
7. Louisville *Herald,* June 13, 1924.
8. *Herald,* February 26 – 27, 1923, front page and regular news, March 11, 1923, June 1, 1923, June 5, 1923, July 4, 1923, September 20 – 22, 1923.
9. *Herald,* June 16 – 17, 1924.
10. Anonymous Interview, October 12, 1975.
11. *Herald,* March 26 – 29, 1924, front page.
12. Anonymous Interview, June 21, 1975.
13. Jefferson County Criminal Court, Case #45115, 1921.
14. Jefferson County Civil Court, Case #155492 (divorce), 1925.
15. *Herald,* July 23, 1924.
16. Civil Case #148505, 1925.
17. Civil Case #148282, 1924.
18. *Herald,* July 19, 1924, front page.
19. *Herald,* August 20, 1923, front page.
20. *Herald,* August 29, 1923, front page.
21. Anonymous Interview, March 9, 1975.
22. *Courier-Journal* and *Herald,* March 1, 1924, front page; *Herald,* December 12, 1924, front page.
23. Criminal Case #44303, 1920.
24. Criminal Case #56500, 1927.
25. Criminal Case #47093, 1922.
26. Criminal Case #49683, 1924.
27. Civil Case #141578, 1924.
28. Civil Case #149688, 1925.
29. Civil Case #144708, 1924.
30. Civil Case #159012, 1925.

Blacks

119

Fifteen percent of the population of the city were native-born blacks.[1] They died of either pneumonia or tuberculosis.[2] In 1924, the healthiest year of the decade, the black birth rate was 16.9 per 1,000 (as compared with the white of 21.9).[3] That same year, their death rate was 21.6 (as compared with the white of 12). In 1921, their birth and death rates had been, respectively, 9 and 20 (the white had been 17 and 12.8).[4]

In 1928, the earliest year for which there are complete police statistics, 822 blacks were arrested for crimes against a person. This total was 34 percent greater than the number of whites (610) arrested for the same crimes. Fourteen percent fewer blacks (1,499) than whites (1,742) were arrested for crimes against property. Six more blacks (60) than whites (54) killed another person. Twenty-nine percent fewer blacks (1,449) than whites (2,047) were arrested for crimes of passion or crimes against "public morals."[5]

A black jugband agreed to play at a picnic at Turner Park on Preston Street Road. When they showed up, they noticed that some of the men who'd hired them were walking around carrying white sheets. By the time they set up, the park was packed with 10,000 men, women, and children, and 300 Klansmen in robes. The band tried, but couldn't play a note. They couldn't even manage "Dixie," their favorite.[6]

Several white people complained to the City Park Department that some black children were playing in a segregated playground in Iroquois Park. Park guards chased them away. A short time later, the guards returned and found the children playing there again. This time there were two black school-teachers with them. The guards accused the teachers of being irresponsible. The teachers became enraged. The guards said they were only doing their job. Then they arrested the teachers and charged them with disorderly conduct. Police kept them in jail for a few hours until they raised bail.[7]

"The white people - they'd call us nigger - nigger - nig -

ger . . . They done taught their kids how to call us nigger . . . They'd take our people, our family, our kin-people would go out there and cook for 'em . . . but they didn't want you to set down at the table with 'em. You'd go to school, get your diploma and everything, come out and have to get in a kitchen or cook instead of being a teacher . . . you'd throw away your time trying to send your child to school, graduate . . . and have to get into a kitchen . . . you'd have to go down to Mississippi, Georgia . . . and you couldn't stay here where you were raised at . . . you couldn't get no jobs teaching here.

"Go to a picture show, you had to go up them steps, had to go down an alley. They'd built it so that you just had to turn right off the street, right around the side; you'd have to go out an alley and up to the third floor, the "Buzzard's Roost" is what they called it—every show in Louisville; and then they'd still call us everything you could name . . .

"The police were against colored people just like everyone else . . . You'd be playing your Victrola or something like that and the police would come and make you shut it off; it was eight, nine o'clock at night, the police walking their beats . . . Most of the colored lived back in the alleys; they didn't live on the streets; we lived back in the alleys . . . The white people had the front part, then they had a garage with two or three rooms just over it that they used to rent to colored . . . I was lucky; I lived on the street, between white people, between York and Breckinridge . . . most of my neighbors were all right, but some of 'em made it so hot for me—I'd have to go to Fifth and Breckinridge to get my water; they had a hydrant out there on the street; we didn't have no running water in the house—I'd go up there to get a bucket of water and sometimes

they'd make me run off and leave my bucket. They'd gang me . . . the colored had gangs and they had gangs; they run each other, it wasn't civilized.

"The white people, if you got on a job, they'd pay the white man more than the colored man . . . I worked for a moving company until I got my experience, then I came out and decided to go for myself . . . That company would scold you and talk stuff to you. They'd try to dog you. They brought all their help up from down South when they moved up here . . . Most all the help moving the furniture and stuff was colored; didn't have no white do that. What two men ought to be carrying, they had us, one of us would be carrying . . . I got tired of being bossed, taking that kind of stuff.

"Bought me a T Model Ford truck. I started out crawling with that old Model T . . . When I got my own truck, I got paid same as the white man . . . I was just a little business, but I moved for a lot of people . . . my name rang a bell with them; they'd look me up if they wanted to move because they appreciated my work . . . I was taking *care* of their furniture . . . I used to work for Mrs. Speed . . . ohhh you wouldn't want to work for no better person. Every time we'd do something for her, four or five of us, she'd give us two-dollar tip apiece instead of them dimes, nickles, and quarters and things . . . She was a *nice* woman.

"I quit school in the seventh grade. I done lost my father; my father died and left me with my mother and grandmother, so I was always the man. My brother, he got drowned when he was nine years old. My sister died of double pneumonia when she was three years old. My father died when he was fifty years old, when I was just eighteen . . . I had some lovely parents. Some lovely good people.

"My wife was a nice woman; she didn't bother me. She wasn't a woman who always had her hand stuck out for money . . . I went to school with her. I'd known all about her before I married her. I'd been raised up with her from a child. So we had it good. We taken life together, one love together till death do us part . . . My wife was a mother's girl and wouldn't leave home . . . Her mother did all the cooking and all the washing, she had six or seven children; she just slaved and killed herself, working for them instead of her husband. I was able to get a place of our own, but my wife wouldn't leave her mother; so that kept me kind of fretted all the time because I wanted to get out and get something of my own . . . I didn't have no privacy or nothing, just one room."[8]

"Archie Bird—states 'this happened on the eighteenth of September between four and five in the morning A.M., at 222 E. Walnut Street, rear, both of them lived there; this is the tenants' house, sixteen families. Bickley he lives on the west side and Sanders lived upstairs, Walter closed the toilet by locking it on his [side], they had some trouble about locking of the toilet and went to see the landlord and the landlord caused Bickley to unlock it; and Bickley told a woman, I will lock it again and he did so which was contrary to the orders of the landlord; the toilet was to be for the use of sixteen families, and not intended for the exclusive use of any tenant; Walter's side of the toilet was locked and John Sanders went down with a hammer to put a chain on the side of the toilet where they lived and which they had been accustomed to using, Walter said what are you making so much noise out there for, John answered him that he did'nt think it ought to disturb him anybody that worked ought to be up, Walter said I don't work and he went

back into the house and came out with his revolver into the yard where Sanders was, John was then standing with his back toward Bickley by the closet door, he then turned to talk to Bickley and Bickley fired one shot and walked back into his room; Sanders didn't fall but stumbled out into the alley and I lost sight of him.' "[9]

"Mattie May Johnson, colored, sixteen years of age . . . 'Reverend Ringle sent for me to come into the office and a Mr. Brown was there. Mr. Ringle told me I was to go with Mr. Brown and we started to his home. We stopped in town to purchase some groceries and on the way out to the house Mr. Brown began asking me questions that I thought were improper. He stopped at another store before reaching the house, to get some bread, and before leaving the car he leaned over and kissed me. After making the purchase Mr. Brown came out and we went onto the house. We went in the back way. He took me into the kitchen and through there into the bedroom. He warned me to be careful and not to let the folks upstairs know I was there. He told me to sit down on the bed, which I did, and he began to pull off his clothes. I took up a piece of newspaper that was lying on the bed and put it before my face so that I could not see him undressing. Clothed only in his underwear he set down in a rocker and pulled me over toward him. When he saw that I would not submit, he put his clothes on and went to the kitchen to do some work. Later he came back and asked whether or not I wanted something to eat. I told him no. Then he came in and asked if I wanted some whiskey or something to drink but I told him no. Then he brought in some fruit and I ate an apple. He handed me the evening paper and asked whether or not I wanted to read it. He sat on the bed and began to talk about me reading novels and love stories, then he went into his office and came back with a book, the pictures in which were unclothed women. He asked me to look at it and when I saw what it was I closed it and handed it back to him. He then left the room and came in later and asked me what was my usual bed time. I told him about nine o'clock and he said it was that time then. He told me to sleep in the big bed and asked me whether or not I wanted him to leave the room while I undressed and I told him of course. He told me he had to wait up awhile because he expected a telegram from Mrs. Brown. About a half hour after I was in bed I heard a tap at the door. I pretended not to hear him and then he came into the room. I never saw what he did because I had my head under the cover. He left the room and sometime later during the night, I do not know just what hour, he came back and awakened me as he was getting into bed. He asked me whether or not I was asleep, I never answered him. Then he began to pull me toward him and I took hold of the springs, but he pulled so hard that I had to turn loose. He pulled up my gown and I started to holler but he put his hand over my mouth. It was then that he forced me to have immoral relations with him. About fifteen minutes later the same offense was committed, the second time.

" 'About six o'clock on Saturday morning I got up and Mr. Brown awakened and asked me whether or not I could light the gas. I told him no and he got up and went to the kitchen and told me how to light the stove. He then went back to bed and told me to call him about eight o'clock. He told me to wash up the kitchen and clean up the dirty dishes that were in the sink, then I could rest until Mrs. Brown came home because he did not know just what work she wanted me to do except take care of the boy.

" 'Mrs. Brown returned sometime during the night on Monday. Then everything went all right until Friday night. It was my duty every night to massage Mrs. Brown's body with cold cream. On Friday night while I was doing this Mr. Brown came into the room dressed in his pajamas and got in bed. Mr. Brown began fingering Mrs. Brown and he took my hands and placed them on various parts of Mrs. Brown's body. Mrs. Brown asked me if I was passionate and made some remarks about it. Mr. Brown took me by the arm and pulled me over toward him and Mrs. Brown took off my bloomers. Then Mr. Brown had immoral relations with me again. Mrs. Brown told me Mr. Brown would do this for me until my fellows from town began to come out and see me and then I could take them upstairs to my room and they could use me there. I told them that I had no sweetheart, that he was dead, and that they could just drop the subject. After this I went to the kitchen, washed, and went to bed.

" 'On Saturday I called Mrs. Ringle and asked if some of the girls could go to the flower show with me and I stopped on Saturday afternoon, after I had been to the flower show, and hinted to Mr. Ringle that I did not want to go back to the Browns'. He told me I must go back but after I told him there was a young man occupying the room next to mine he said I had to go back that night but he would write Mr. Brown telling him I could not stay there but he would give him no reasons why. On Saturday night when I went back to Mrs. Brown's I told her I would have to leave and this made her very angry.' ''[10]

104424

One night when Leonard Truit was thirty-five years old, God told him that He had singled him out for death. He began to scream. People became frightened and called the police. An officer named Lawless tried to arrest him. Truit ran into the middle of Ninth and Broadway and shouted up to God: "You made me live for you, and now you want me to die for you." Lawless tried to grab him again, but Truit threw him off. A hundred men, white and black, stood and waited. Lawless got angry and killed him.[11]

". . . I left from Louisville on the Day election. As I did not want to haveing trouble with Boy cription will, as he is a witness against James Waite I and my Husband was eating at the second table from the Door when the trouble started with Haze and Robert Johns I now that this Boy cription Will was not in that Restiraint the trouble started between Robert Johns and Haze. Mr. Hill Son didont saying thig untill they started licks and he ask them not to start anything in here. He told them that the old man dident low iny coursin of swaren in the prisemises.

"He said You all will hafter to go out doors and settle your argement, He forther said you two gentlement read the sines on the wall there were Robert Johns told James Waite the Hell with you and your sines both. Farther-more you son of Bitch put me out and then started with his knifeout and started at a Boy that name is George Towns. He cut at George and George run and then turn on James Waite the same night Waite run up in his kitchen and said not come up here. Me and my Husband run out the door still hering Waite say dont come up here the last of it I saw of Robert Johns he was still advancin still toward Waite and wee did not more than git off the sidewalk be-

for the gun fired. There where we met Scription Will coming toward Seader Street the next day we saw him he noed more than iny body. He fell out with me and my husband because we told him he aught to be ashamed of hisself because he knowed he was a lieing and the nearer the trial come off they begin to threaten our life, I told my husband not to get in to iny trouble with them Dope themes. We would leave the city. We are liven at 5101 John Street, but we are working across the river at New Port. What I have written you in this letter is true port course as I say I would like to be theire but as well as we Both nows them Dope themes it would pay us both to keep away from there this is my evidence I am swarin to the present of a notery."[12]

"Q. 'Were you present?' / A. 'I was. There was a good many there.'
Q. 'Did you see the deceased come in?' / A. 'He was in there when I come. He look like he had been drinking a little.'
Q. 'Did he at any time make any threats toward the defendant?' / A. 'Yes, sir, the way it first started we was playing blackjack and the fellow was dealing the cards, and this fellow had nine chips out there, and he so wanted to get everybody around the table, and when he got to him he turned his hand over and he didn't have but seventeen, and the deal had eighteen, and he reached out and got them, and at that time Sam reached and got all the chips.'
Q. 'He tried to break up the game?' / A. 'Yes, sir, and we all tried to show him he was in wrong, and then he got sore. He stood there a while, and after a while he asked him to push him over four chips and he lost them, and after a while he asked him to pitch him four more, and he did, and then he

asked him for some more and he pitched him two, and he lost them and he asked him for some more and he said he could not give him them. He said: "If I start over there after you, you cant keep me from coming over there. Some of these other black sons-of-bitches may keep me from coming, but you won't." '

Q. 'How close were you standing to Bet at the time?' / A. 'My back to the wall, the second man from him.'

Q. 'Did he go in Bet's direction?' / A. 'He went to another game where they were playing and then turned back and put his hand in here.'

Q. 'What did he say?' / A. 'He said: "Well, I will see you tomorrow and tell you the same thing." And he aimed to turn around.'

Q. 'To face the defendant?' / A. 'Yes, sir.'

Q. 'Did he call him any names?' /A. 'I heard him call him a frog eyed son-of-a-bitch.' "[13]

"he drink whiskey and got drunk and gambled; run around with other women and use Dope. He wasted his money and spent it foolishly, his taxicab bill for the month of May 1922 was sixty-five dollars and this was for joy riding. he took a diamond ring that did not belong to him but belong to my sister, and pond it and spent the money on other women, then he wrote me a letter and said I could find his body in the Ohio River and his clothes would be found behind the racing derby at Fontaine Ferry Park. I found his clothes there and dragged the river for his body . . . he of course finally run off and left me."[14]

"Walter Larkins (1438 South Seventh): 'I know this fellow Davis and I was with him Saturday night two weeks ago. We both slept in the poolroom and when I woke up in the morning I found Davis dead. I met him about three o'clock in the afternoon and we went up town and bummed around and then we came back and went over to Mr. Hopkins and got a half pint of whiskey and I took a couple of drinks and he took a couple of drinks and about eight or nine o'clock that night we went over to the poolroom and stayed there about a half of an hour and then went to the back of the place and fell asleep. When I woke up Davis was dead. I didn't see him drink anything else that day. We paid a dollar and a quarter for the pint of whiskey. It made me sick and I vomited and threw it all up and then it was all right.' "[15]

Max Head was a bellhop at the Henry Watterson Hotel. He carried bags and sold something labeled either "Cedar Brook" or "Old Buck Tanner" for $8.50 a pint. The stuff was low-grade moonshine, called "red liquor" after the toxic dye that colored it. It cost about seventy-five cents to make a pint. Head tried to sell it to some Prohibition agents on Thanksgiving night and got himself arrested.[16]

221
ASSOCIATED
FIRST NATIONAL PICTURES
OF KENTUCKY AND TENNESSEE

"I got a job bellhopping at the Seelbach Hotel . . . You

didn't make no money. You had to pay the head bellman fifty cents a day to let you work . . . The hotel didn't pay us nothing. The people would tip us a dime, maybe fifteen cent, never hardly got a quarter for a tip . . . I was working at the hotel when Graham Brown, the man that built the Brown Hotel, stopped in the Seelbach during Derby Week; and he was cutting pillows and throwing them out on Fourth Street. So the man that owned the hotel, Otto Seelbach, sent the houseman up there and told him that if he didn't quit cutting and throwing them pillows out on Fourth Street—see they were flying from Walnut Street all the way down to Fourth and Broadway—that he was gonna put him outa the hotel. And Graham Brown told this houseman, he say, 'You go back and tell Otto Seelbach that he ain't got nothing but a *dump* to live in, and five years from today I'm gonna have a *hotel* in this town.' And the next year, he built the Brown Hotel.

"Most of the working people went to eat at Burkhart's . . . to get their beans. Bowl of beans. Beans, root beer, pig feet, and hot dog. A white guy named Burkhart owned it. Wasn't no other place you could set down and eat if you was colored. Wasn't a place on Fourth Street you could set down. You had root beer. A big old glass of root beer for a nickle. A bowl of beans for a dime and three or four slices of bread with it and a nickle frankfort. That's all you'd want for your lunch.

"In 1926, I went to Brown and Williamson to get a job, but they didn't work no colored but porters. They didn't have no colored working there at all, just the porters—and they didn't have but twelve of them and they didn't pay but sixteen dollars a week—big money then. There wasn't nobody making over ten or twelve a week—and *no* jobs, hardly. Wasn't too many factories with colored work. Fifteen and twenty dollars a week was top bread . . . I had to pay five dollars a week for my board and room; and I would send five dollars a week *home* to Commerce, Georgia, to my mother.

"I lived at Thirty-sixth and Hale. Dirt streets down there. Weren't no sidewalks; weren't no streets. Old man Jackson, my neighbor, was a jack-leg preacher and a blacksmith and stuff like that . . . There was a place called the Climax Night Club . . . They'd bootleg some 'splo—some white whisky. You would get a table and a little pitcher of whisky, mix it with some pop . . . Some of the people dressed nice, and some of 'em didn't. If you was sharp, you wore a box-back coat with P.I. shoes—light tan—and sharp toes that would look up at you . . . Women wore white boots all the way up with short dresses. Spool heel boots . . . We used to go to the Pythian Building for dance up on the roof garden of the Pythian. You couldn't rent no place in the white place to have no dance."[17]

R. A. Wathen, the manager of the Louisville Auto Supply Company, hired Will Smith as a night watchman. Smith got drunk and threatened to shoot Wathen when he tried to get back into his own store. Wathen called the police; Smith held them off until he was wounded in the arm and leg. He said he'd only done what was right. "When I get hired as a night watchman to keep men out, I keep them out."[18]

"We was raised on the farm, this was in Georgia, and you didn't have no cotton, you didn't have much money. My sister and her husband, they moved to Louisville and they were making pretty good money; they was making twenty dollars and some odd a week, and they was writing to me 'Ohhh, I'm making so much and so much.' So I said to my wife, I'm going up and see what's going on. A friend of mine met me at Seventh Street Station. That was in 1923 . . . We lived in Little Africa. We didn't go no further than Sixth or Seventh Street, there wasn't nothing past there for us . . . There was a bunch of us Georgia niggers and Alabama and Mississippi niggers. The Kentuckians wouldn't have us, so finally we got together and built a church in 1925 . . .

"Reynolds Metal Company was the first job that I had; if you're making forty cents an hour, you're making big money. I had to work at night, from eleven to seven, working hard all night long . . . I didn't have no trouble all the time I was there, twenty-one years . . . My first job was unloading cars. We put lead shipped in from St. Louis with tin from China—it looked like gold—great big heavy blocks of tin, shipped in from China, taking the metal out and stacking it in the shop.

"I fractured my back on a Saturday morning . . . I wanted to make some money. We had to stack cross-ties for the railroads so they could be treated and shipped out. Something told me not to go to work that day; the Master spoke to me and said not to go to work that morning, but my wife and kids were in Atlanta, so I said I got to go to work, I got to go to work so I can send them money so they can come home. I like to got killed that morning."[19]

Fred P Simms: "Saturday December fifth I was coming down the steps of my store and this fellow came up and asked me about garnisheeing him and I said come up to my office and I would talk to him about it and as I turned around this fel-

low had a big piece of iron and hit me over the head with it and cracked my head. If it hadn't been for my hat it probably would have killed me."[20]

A judge sent Charles Cockey Reed to the federal prison in Atlanta for three years and fined him $3,010. The $3,000 was for dealing drugs, and the ten dollars was for coming into court smoking a cigarette. Reed wrote out a check on the spot.[21]

George Scott complained that he'd been beaten by two cops after he refused to pay them the eight dollars they always collected every Sunday to stay away from the crap game he ran in his pool hall. The same day Scott said he was beaten, police raided crap games in two other pool halls and arrested 110 blacks. Four days after that, they arrested 200 more.[22]

Police raided a pool hall looking for a crap game. They didn't find the game, but one of them caught a whiff of C.C. Cook. They arrested Cook and charged him with robbing the house of Mrs. J.P. Van Winkle, who had just returned from a Cuban vacation with some exotic perfume in bottles shaped like dice.[23]

Big Hand George was a dealer who'd killed two men during a business argument on Liberty Street in 1922. The cops arrested him, then let him go. They paid him a visit a year later. He kept on smiling until they found his stash underneath a window behind a spring panel. George had been holding $1,600 worth of morphine and cocaine. He'd been dealing ounces of morphine for forty-eight dollars, two-grain caps of it for fifty cents, and powders called "decks" for seventy-five cents.[24]

A white woman named Mrs. Jones said that she'd returned from feeding her pet chicken to find a "yellow Negro" with a razor, hiding in her clothes closet. The man threatened to cut her throat, and then asked her where she'd hidden her jewels. She struggled with him and he ran.[25]

Herald Jackson came to Louisville from Roanoke, Virginia, in 1922. For a year he stole fine jewelry from the nice people who lived in Crescent Hill. He did it with care and discretion. When the cops caught him, he told them that if they behaved themselves, he'd save the city the expense of a trial by accepting a one-year sentence. He wasn't treated as well as he'd expected. When he came to trial two weeks later, he held his head down and told the judge he'd take twenty years without a jury. The judge would have given it to him if a dozen of the people he'd robbed hadn't said he didn't deserve it. Jackson lifted his head up and told the judge he'd done it to support his wife and two children. He said he'd taken orders from two other men. The judge let him off with ten.[26]

"I worked for this old man. I valeted for him. When he was twenty-one, his daddy gave him $1 million and told him, 'Son, you're on your own.' So he retired. He made himself some investments, and that's all he did. He was hard to work for and hard to get along with, *but* he'd go out of his way and do people favors.

"He tried to be bad with me sometime. See, I bought a Chrysler in 1926. He fired me when I bought that car, 'cause he didn't want me to have no car . . . Niggers didn't have no cars . . . Servants stayed on the place. They didn't have but one or two days off in the week . . . It wasn't paying you enough money, but you weren't supposed to leave the place. When I worked for this guy, I was supposed to be off every Thursday and every other Sunday . . . but instead of letting me off in the morning, he wouldn't let me off until two o'clock. See, on my day off he'd always play sick . . . I always had to take his breakfast up to him, draw his bath water, and put his things out so he could *shave*, and get his clothes out and keep his shoes shined and all that kinda crap . . . So I *told* him one day. We got into it, and I just quit. Then he got sick and wanted me to come back and work for him, but I wouldn't work for him. For the *same* money, no more. I made him have an understanding that I'm gonna be off at a certain time—'if you're sick, I'm going; if you ain't sick, I'm going.' But sometime, he'd say, 'Frederick, why'd you slip off for yesterday.' Like I was supposed to be there. And I said, 'You know my day off . . . you better get your somebody 'cause I'm going . . .'

"He had two chauffeurs, but he liked me to drive—why I didn't know. He'd make out like I could drive better and this, that, and the other and always have some kinda excuse.

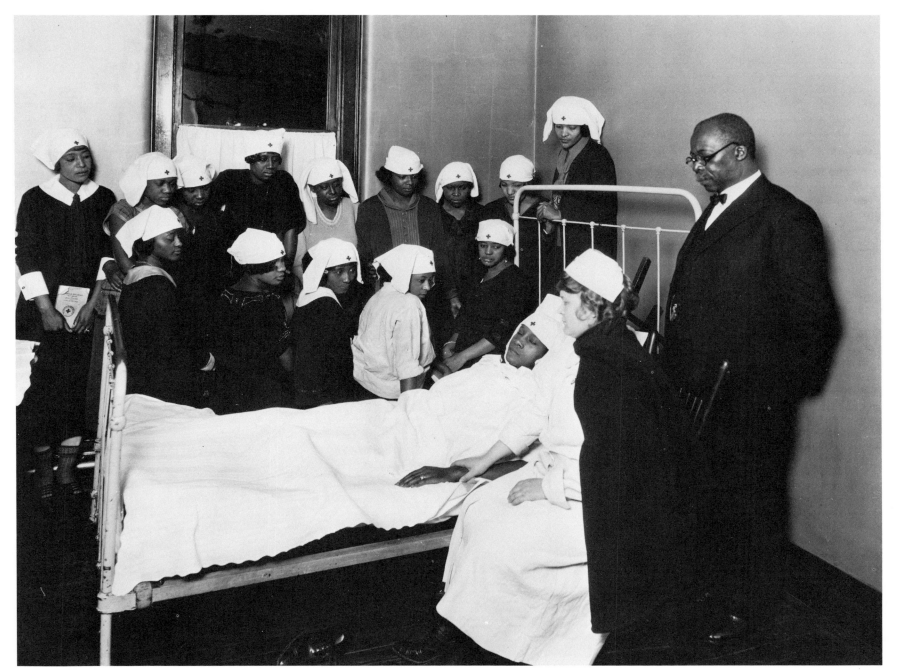

143

143

When he got into the car, I'd ask him—the rest of 'em that was driving him was afraid of him—I ask him, 'Now, Sir, where are you going? Are you going to the office or are you going to the club?' He never would tell you where to go. Sometimes he'd say, 'Well, I'm going to the office.' I start taking him to the office, he'd say, 'Hell! I want to go to the club!' I say, 'Now you say you told me you was going to the office.' And he done called in and told the stenographer to tear it up, 'cause he was gonna be in in a few minutes! Well, she set there and wait and he wouldn't go to that office sometimes for maybe a *week*. He'd go over to the club, start playing cards, playing poker.

"He'd done blown a lot of his money, gambling it off. He was a heck of a poker player. When he go to New York, them people would beat him out of a *whole* lot of money up there. His *friends* would. They'd plot on him. He set down and start playing cards at eleven o'clock in the morning; he play cards till twelve o'clock at night, and he could tell you what everybody held and what everybody fell with. You couldn't beat him if you played on the square.

"We would have a good time. We would go down to Florida; we'd take a nurse with us; we'd get a nice stack. Hardly had nothing to do but pull corn every day. When we come back, his wife would get jealous of me and the old man. When we came home, she tell all the help, 'Don't y'all wait on him. Let Fred wait on him.' Old man ring the bell, wouldn't nobody wait on him. Old man would call 'em all up there, up to his room, say, 'Listen, when that bell rings, if Fred don't answer, somebody better answer because I'm paying everybody in this house. I'm the boss. I pay everybody.' "[27]

Notes

1. *Compilation of Basic Data, Economic and Social,* anonymous unpublished manuscript, 1933 (Kentucky Room, Louisville Public Library).
2. *Ibid.*
3. *Ibid.*
4. *Report,* U.S. Bureau of Census, 1929, and *Annual Report,* Louisville Board of Health, 1921.
5. Louisville Department of Police, *1928 Annual Report.*
6. Louisville *Herald,* August 10, 1924.
7. *Herald,* June 14,1924.
8. Anonymous Interview, November 12, 1975.
9. Jefferson County Criminal Court, Case #43366, 1919.
10. Criminal Case #58000, 1927.
11. *Herald,* March 7, 1923.
12. Criminal Case #45417, 1921.
13. Criminal Case #44328, 1920.
14. Jefferson County Civil Court, Case #131374, 1922.
15. Criminal Case #46254, 1922.
16. *Herald,* December 1,1923.
17. Anonymous Interview, December 10, 1975.
18. *Herald,* March 2, 1924.
19. Anonymous Interview, November 11, 1975.
20. Criminal Case #52734, 1925.
21. *Herald,* April 10, 1924.
22. *Herald,* May 21, 1924, May 26, 1924.
23. *Herald,* June 27, 1924.
24. *Herald,* August 23, 1923.
25. *Herald,* July 28, 1924.
26. *Herald,* June 25, 1923.
27. Anonymous Interview, April 7, 1975.

POWER

"WOES OF LOVESICK BREWSTER AND HIS MIL-LIONS / Wife Says He May Marry The $250,000 Love Nest Beauty, But She'll Ruin Him First . . ."[1]

"WHEN MULTI-MILLIONAIRES 'STEP-OUT' / Beating Boredom Al Fresco At Its Own Game By Taking Up The Tasks Of Humble Toilers Is The Latest Fad Of A Jaded '400' "[2]

"HAS THE '400' FOUND A NEW WAY TO SCOLD ITS MODERN BEAUTIES? / How The Latest Social Dictum Is Chastizing The Butterflies Who Changed Their Long Faces for Short Skirts"[3]

"NO END TO THE TURMOIL OVER THIS DASHING DON JUAN / The Coal Baron's Son Got Back From Princeton And In Four Years Bumped Into Four Divorce Suits, Three Secret Marriages, And Two Charges of Bigamy"[4]

"ADVENTURES OF THE CUTEST FLAPPER AND THE RICHEST CADET / How The Date Of Millionaire Statler's Foster Son Ran Into A Whirligig Of Smash Ups, Flying Fists, And A St. Vitus Dance Defense"[5]

"SAYS HE: SHE SENT ME, MY SPATS, AND MY MON-OCLE TO JAIL / SAYS SHE: HE MADE $400 A WEEK AND ALL I GOT WAS STOCKINGS"[6]

"Went to Georgetown College, Washington, two years and then to Center College, specialized in mathematics. Did not graduate in either place. Then was manager for steel plant in Brownsboro, owned by his father, for a time but they finally sold the plant out . . . Claims that the doctors gave him morphine for over a year and that he did not know he was taking it. This was for a nervous condition which was present during and following an attack of mountain fever, which was a rare case and for the observation of which people came for miles around . . . He has taken the drug for about twenty-two years. During that time has never been off from it for any appreciable length of time. Has taken as much as sixty grains of morphine and the same amount of cocaine in one dose. He has taken any number of cures and has always gone back to the drug; has taken all preparations, such as cocaine, morphine, hasheesh, heroin, smoking opium in pipes for the sensation. Claims he never feels any amount of energy to perform any work unless he is under the influence of the drug."[7]

Blackey Barlow's father sent him a check once a month. When it came, Blackey went out and scored cocaine and morphine. He and his girlfriend shot up and snorted for the rest of the month and then waited for the next check. He didn't do much except stay high and keep a diary: ". . . as usual, the more money, the more junk . . . Financial affairs of an international character are subject to conditions that will be most unfortunate for certain interests guided by the planet Jupiter. Mars, afflicting the ruling sign of Italy, gives warning of seriously disturbing influences in that country. Sweden and the Transvaal will have a year of many anxieties and certain trouble if the signs are read right. Religious differences will be marked in the United States and prejudices will be fanned . . . Propaganda of the most insidious sort will gain wide credence . . . I must get out of this dump . . ."[8]

One hundred thousand people came to Louisville to celebrate the Golden Jubilee Anniversary of the Kentucky Derby. The very rich came in private cars attached to seventeen special trains. The TC-3, a semirigid dirigible, landed near the track at noon, before the race began. Mr. S. George and Mrs. W. K. Vanderbilt watched from private boxes. August Belmont sat near them, and near him sat the Whitneys, Charles Dana Gibson, J. S. Cosden, and Charles H. Sabin.

"Mrs. George Andres Duerbacher wore a gown of midnight blue charmeuse combined with powder blue Georgette beaded with bronze and coral beads, and a black Milan hat faced with powder blue Georgette trimmed with flat roses of pastel shades, black threaded lace . . . The Marquise de Charette wore a Lanvin green flannel cape dress trimmed in burnt orange and a black cloche with a stiff gold ribbon band, and carried a mah jong parasol . . . Mrs. Harry Heath wore a white Kasha cloth sports dress trimmed with silk braid, white sports hat, sports coat of green ripple cloth trimmed with summer ermine . . . Mrs. Edward Altsheler wore a black Poiret twill, long black coat trimmed in caracul, and a hat with red flowers . . . Miss Blanche Bailey wore a tweed tailored suit, with handkerchief of King Tut silk . . . Miss Ruth Kammerer wore a dress of white flannel braided in Chinese yellow, and a black hat trimmed with yellow flowers, and choker beads of Chinese yellow . . . Mrs. Charles Marshall wore a dress of white Canton crepe banded in black romaine crepe, and a coat of black romaine with ermine collar . . ."[9]

Black Gold won. He was owned by Osage Indians from Tulsa; they'd named him after the oil that had made them rich.[10]

Robert Bingham has already been mentioned as patron and business associate of Jim Brown. Between 1916 and 1924, Bingham changed from a corporate lawyer who had once been appointed mayor and later judge into a newspaper publisher who was to be named ambassador. He inhabited a class whose members sometimes behaved like a family, sometimes like the citizens of a small town, and sometimes like the crew of a ship. Within this small world, fortune changed as much because of love and acquaintance as because of luck or circumstance. Robert Bingham found his particular fortune wedged between the sudden death of his second wife and a quarrel between two brothers after the death of their father.

Bingham was born six years after the end of the Civil War. His father directed a military academy that the family had founded in 1793.[11] The Colonel had educated his own son and then sent him to the University of North Carolina in 1887. When Robert was a sophomore, he met Mary Lilly Kenan. His father and her father had been friends in Wilmington. Robert courted her, but when they graduated, she went off to a finishing school and he went to Munich to study art. He returned to study law, first at the University of Virginia, and then at the University of Louisville. When he was twenty-five, he married a Louisville woman named Eleanor Miller. He practiced corporate law, raised three children, and moved responsibly from one civic appointment to the next. In the meantime, Mary Lilly had turned thirty, and made the acquaintance of Henry M. Flagler during a vacation. Mr. Flagler had helped John D. Rockefeller refine oil in Cleveland many years before Mary was born. When he and Mary were introduced, he was no older than seventy-four and worth not more than $210 million. He was a director and principal stockholder of Standard Oil, and was a builder and owner of the Florida East Coast Railway. He also owned a good deal of Florida real estate, and quite a few members of the Florida House of Representatives. When his second wife went mad, he had a bill introduced that made four years of insanity grounds for divorce. Ten days after the bill became law, he married Mary Kenan. When he died in 1913, he left her everything. She became the richest forty-four-year-old widow in America.

The same year that Mary Kenan lost her husband, Robert Bingham lost his wife. She died when her brother drove his car across the tracks, in front of a train.[12] Bingham waited a decent interval and then resumed the courtship of Mary Kenan that he had begun twenty-five years before. Her family was not terribly pleased when he proposed marriage in 1916.

He tried to reassure them by signing a marriage contract that separated his money from hers. Mary did her best by announcing that when she died she planned to leave $75 million to her family and $60 million to her niece Louise.

No one came to the wedding but Louise.

Nine months later, Mary went to see a doctor about her heart and a lawyer about her will. By July, she was dead of myocarditis. Her family thought she had been murdered. They were sure that Bingham had talked her into changing her will in his favor, and then poisoned her. They had her dug up and dissected.[13] A New York pathologist investigated her heart and kidneys. Private detectives broke into her doctor's office in Louisville and stole his records. Every newspaper in the city defended Bingham. They blamed the whole episode on the nasty selfishness of the Kenan family. The probate court in New York agreed. On July 28, the codicil of Mary Kenan's will was decided in her husband's favor. Bingham inherited $5 million worth of stock in such companies as Standard Oil and Union Tankline.[14] Fidelity-Columbia Trust Company administered the estate.[15]

The same day that Bingham inherited the money, he bought the Louisville *Times* and the Louisville *Courier-Journal* from the Haldeman family for more than $1 million. The *Times* was nothing more than a pleasant metropolitan daily, but the *Courier* had been the Democratic voice of the entire region since Reconstruction. Walter Haldeman, its publisher, and Henry Watterson, its editor, had spoken for the political economy of the New South for thirty years. Walter Haldeman died in 1902 and left the papers to his two sons, William and Bruce, and his daughter Isabelle. William was the oldest. He had enlisted in the Confederate Army when he was fifteen and fought in the battles of Chickamauga and Missionary Ridge. After the war, he had been a surveyor and then a lawyer.[16] His father made him general manager of the *Courier* in 1886, and, in his will, named him editor of the *Times*. His younger brother Bruce had been born in the second year of the war. He attended the University of Virginia for two years, and then was shunted by his father from one business management position to another inside the papers.[17] His father's will made him president of the newspaper companies. Fourteen years later William wanted to retire, but Bruce didn't. William settled the argument by filing suit to remove Bruce from office. He succeeded with the help of his attorney, Robert Bingham, who bought the papers a year later. Bruce and his wife eventually went off on a round-the-world cruise, and William spent the rest of his life raising money to build a monument to Jefferson Davis. He died in 1924, while watching a horse race at Churchill Downs.[18]

Robert Bingham waited another decent interval and then married Ailleen Muldoon, another widow.[19] Her husband had been Byron Hilliard, an eminently genteel stockbroker who was senior partner in a Louisville firm his father had founded forty years before. Bingham may very well have been one of his clients.[20] The couple got married in London, under special license granted by the Archbishop of Canterbury. It was Bingham's last marriage. During the rest of the decade, he occupied himself with organizing an interstate tobacco cooperative, and hunting grouse once a year on his 300,000-acre plantation in Georgia. He established the first radio station in Kentucky, and sat on the boards of the Louisville & Nashville Railroad and the Liberty Bank and Trust Company.[21] When Jim Brown went under in 1930, Bingham personally guaranteed 50 percent of every Christmas account in the First National Bank of Kentucky.[22] His papers supported Roosevelt in the 1932 election, and the President repaid the favor by naming him ambassador to Great Britain.[23] He died at his post in 1937, wearing a face that had come to resemble Woodrow Wilson's.

Frederick Sackett was the Republican equivalent of Robert Bingham. Like Bingham, he began the process of becoming an ambassador by marrying the right woman. He had been born in 1868 in Providence, Rhode Island. His father owned mills that made paper and woolens, and his grandfather had manufactured jewelry on almost the same scale that others manufactured shoes.[24] Sackett graduated from Brown and then Harvard Law School. He went west to Ohio, to practice law and look for an opportunity. He found it in 1898 in Cincinnati, where he met and married a woman named Olive Speed.

Olive Speed was the daughter of James Breckinridge Speed, who was the son of William Pope Speed, who was the brother of Joshua and James, who were altogether only three of the eleven children that Judge John had fathered after he settled in Louisville in 1810. The Speed family had been Republican since the day Joshua had sold Abraham Lincoln a set of junk furniture on credit for his law office in Springfield, Illinois. Joshua's brother James had been Lincoln's attorney general in 1864 and had presided over the early amnesties that had first been offered to Southern gentlemen of wealth and influence. Two years later, James had resigned after he and Congress and the Secretary of War had collided with Andrew Johnson, a Democrat from Tennessee who had no sympathy with Northern businessmen. Long before that happened, James's brother, William Pope, had married Mary Shallcross, whose family owned a fleet of Ohio and Mississippi River steamboats. Mary had borne James Breckinridge and then died young. When the Civil War began, the boy enlisted in the Union Army. He fought until 1865; then he returned to Louisville and grew rich. He founded the Speed and Louisville Cement companies; he became president of the Louisville Railway Company, which had originally been founded and owned by two Du Pont brothers; and he owned and then sold the Ohio Valley Telephone Company, which eventually became part of the Cumberland Telephone. When he died in 1912 some people said he had been one of the richest men in America.[25]

Once Sackett became a Speed he went to work. He began as vice president of the Louisville Cement Company and the Speed Realty Company. He became president of the Black Star Coal Company of Bell County, and the vice president of the Beaver Dam and North Jellicoe Coal companies, all controlled by the family. Between 1907 and 1912, he served as president of the Louisville Gas and Electric Company, and sat on the boards of the American Tar Products Company and the Fidelity-Columbia Bank. He did as much and perhaps more than J.W. Barr to convince the government to build Camp Taylor near the city. The Louisville chamber of commerce, known as the Board of Trade, thanked him for it in 1917 by electing him president. That same year, the government appointed him Federal Food Administrator for Kentucky.

For two years, Sackett explained to the people of the state whatever the Federal Food Administrator, Herbert Hoover, told him to. He issued directives that read like crazy puzzles: "Monday is a wheatless day with one wheatless meal; Tuesday is a meatless day with a wheatless evening meal; Wednesday is a wheatless day with one meatless meal; Thursday has a meatless meal with a wheatless evening meal; Friday has a meatless meal with a wheatless evening meal; Saturday is a porkless day with a wheatless evening meal; and Sunday has a meatless meal with a wheatless evening meal."[26] He used his imagination to enforce the rules once he published them. When sugar was rationed, he ordered that any waiter who served a customer more than two cubes was to be fired, and then banned from ever working in a restaurant again.[27] He printed special "food slacker cards" and ordered restaurants to hand them to those customers who wanted wheat-cakes on Wednesdays or pork chops on Sundays. If the customer signed,

he was served and then reported. The card read: "This certifies that I, _____, a citizen of the United States, residing at _____ street, State of Kentucky, wish to record my protest of meatless and wheatless days . . . I am not in favor of the conversion of foods of any kind or in any way for the use of United States Soldiers or allies in Europe, although I realize that food may win the war . . . witness: _____; signed: _____."[28] Every week, he published a price list that appealed to housewives to "place their cooking stoves on the firing line for democracy against autocracy."[29]

Herbert Hoover never forgot him. In 1924, Sackett was elected to the Senate for a six-year term. In 1927, when Hoover was Secretary of Commerce, they conferred about Red Cross Flood Relief. In 1930, when Hoover was President, he remembered what Sackett had done to win the war at home, and sent him to Germany as ambassador to preside over the consequences. Sackett lasted for three months after Hitler became Chancellor in 1933.[30]

Notes

1. Louisville *Herald, Sunday Feature*, February 3, 1924.
2. *Herald, Sunday Feature*, July 13, 1924.
3. *Herald, Sunday Feature*, January 20, 1924.
4. *Herald, Sunday Feature*, August 24, 1924.
5. *Herald, Sunday Feature*, December 14, 1924.
6. *Herald, Sunday Feature*, December 28, 1924.
7. Central State Hospital, Clinical Records, Case #21409, 1927.
8. *Herald*, January 11, 1923.
9. *Herald*, May 18, 1924.
10. Louisville *Courier-Journal*, May 18, 1924.
11. *New York Times*, May 9, 1927.
12. *Courier-Journal*, April 28, 1913.
13. *Courier-Journal*, July 17, 1918.
14. *Herald*, June 14, 1924.
15. *Courier-Journal*, April 29, 1923.
16. J.S. Johnson, ed., *Memorial History of the City of Louisville* (Chicago: American Biographical Publishing Co., 1896).
17. *Ibid.*
18. *Herald*, October 28, 1924.
19. *Herald*, August 21, 1924.
20. Louisville *Times* and *Herald*, March 20, 1922; *Courier-Journal*, March 9, 1922, January 30, 1927.
21. *New York Times*, February 24, 1933.
22. *Lexington Herald*, February 24, 1933.
23. Louisville *Herald Post*, March 31, 1933.
24. *The National Cyclopedia of American Biography*, Vol. E (New York: James T. White and Co., 1938), p. 45.
25. James B. Speed, *James B. Speed: A Personality* (Louisville; Morton & Co., 1914); Louisville Press Club, *Who's Who in Louisville* (Louisville: Anzeiger Press, 1912); Kathleen Jennings, *Louisville's First Families* (Louisville: Standard Printing Co., 1920); *Courier-Journal*, February 16, 1924, May 19, 1941; *Louisville Post*, December 29, 1924.
26. *Herald*, January 29, 1918.
27. *Herald*, June 10, 1918.
28. *Herald*, January 5, 1918.
29. *Ibid.*
30. Louisville *Courier-Journal* and *Times* and *Lexington Herald*, May 19–20, 1941.

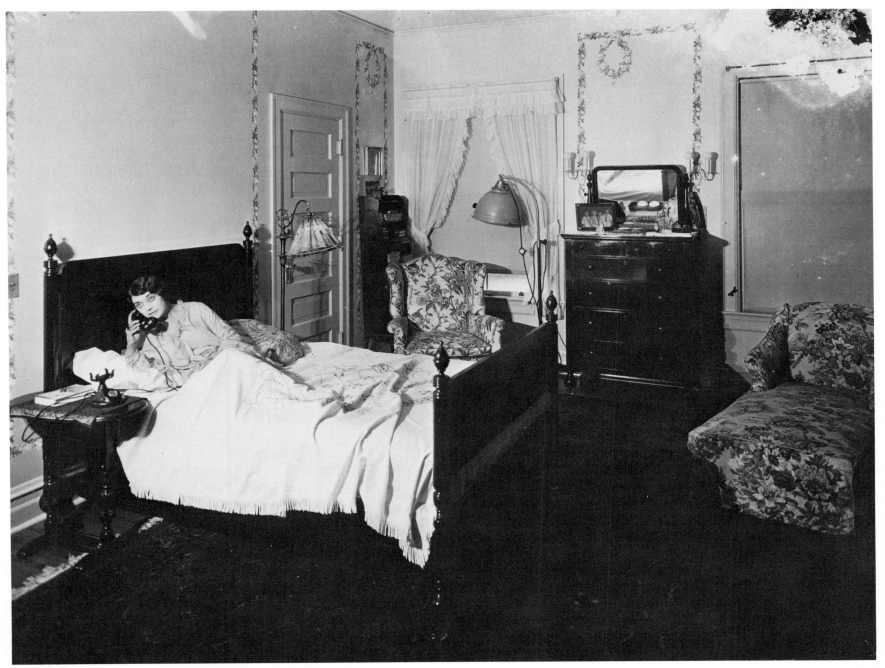

Visions

170

ONE DAY SALE SATURDAY

F.W. WOOLWORTH CO. STORE
INCORPORATED

Our Highest Price
10¢   10¢

ONE DAY SA

Nationally
Advertised
TOILET
ARTICLES
of
Known Quality
and
Exceptional Values
Our Highest Price
10¢

Each 10¢

F.W. WOOLWORTH CO.

178

"THE WASP"

EQUIPMENT

1 MACHINE GUN
3 SAWED OFF SHOT GUNS
4 REVOLVERS
5 TEAR GAS GUNS
3 TEAR GAS BILLIES
BULLET PROOF GLASS
50 ROUNDS EACH
FOR ALL
ARMS ABOARD

"THE LIFE OF
AN EMPLOYEE-
A SACRED
TRUST"

ARMORED CAR COMPANY

THE WASP

Jacob Merz went crazy when he was fifty-four. The

authorities stood him up in front of a judge and jury and asked him to explain.

He said it all began when he was eighteen. He lived in a rough part of town called "The Point." One night the Jesse James gang and part of the Younger crowd rode through and kidnapped him. They took him over to Indiana and forced him to rob a bank. Then Jesse James shot him through the heart. "It was a week before I was able to leave my bed after this shooting, and a week before I was myself again." Once he was back on his feet, he told the U.S. government about the robbery. They admired him so much that they made him a U.S. marshal. He went out and arrested a lot of people, but there were some that were still after him. He told the judge he'd been married three or four times, one time to Jack Dempsey's mother. He used to do some prize fighting himself when he was younger. John L. Sullivan had been his trainer. He'd gone by the name of "Kid" Roberts and knocked out Bob Fitzsimmons in New York in eight rounds. After that, he'd given John Smith, "now known as Tom Mix, to the motion picture world." He admitted he'd got into trouble when he was thirty-nine. The criminal court had tried him for murder and sentenced him to be hanged. They'd put a rope around his neck and were getting ready to spring the trap when someone remembered that the real murderer was a blond. He said they must not have noticed that his "crowning glory was dark."[1]

He'd done a lot of reading.

"SCIENCE'S NEWEST DARING ATTEMPT TO PROBE THE MYSTERY OF MARS / Huge Light Beams . . . Gigantic Flashes of Light. Reflected From Alpine Snow Are To Be Projected Towards Mars . . . / A Martian Monster, All Head And Brains And Tentacles, Attacking An Earth Woman Who Has Landed On The Planet . . ."[2]

"Claims that when a young boy he was sitting on his grandfather's lap and he looked up at the moon and saw the man in the moon smoking a pipe. A few years ago he got so he could not work—father tried to induce him to work but when he did this he told his father he was going to jump in the river. Along about this time he was standing outside their home one evening, looked up at the moon and the man in the moon was singing—it was the prettiest song he had ever heard—the song seemed to come through the top of his head. Then something shot through various parts of his body, warm like—like a lot of warm strings. Something shot through his arm and from there to his leg and something raised up on his thigh like a goose, burning. Then something began to grow on his left hand like an eagle and it had an eye, an ear, and he thinks this talked to him. All of this originated from the man in the moon." [3]

"SCIENCE NOW PROVES THAT 'SUNSPOTS' CAUSE OUR WOES / How The World-Old Solar Superstitions About Wars, Plagues, Revolutions And Everyday Ills Have Received Astonishing Support From Modern Astronomers"[4]

"Began to believe and now thinks that there is certain amount of energy in circulating water, that people throw their thoughts represented by their voices into the water, if this is strong enough you hear the voices. These voices influenced him, and to an extent he felt compelled to do things he did not want to do . . . At times these things have so strong an action on him that it goes up to the top of his head, down through his body so that his body moves involuntarily . . . Thinks he may be one of a million who do not know the working of energy in the water but he is getting educated every day. This to him is a mysterious thing; a peculiar state which he does not know the entire working just yet."[5]

"SCIENCE SPRINGS A '4th DEGREE' THOUGHT RADIO / A New Machine That Will Read . . . Minds Exactly As Receiving Sets Catch And Amplify Sounds In The Air / . . . Human Thoughts Are Caught By Delicate Wires Corresponding To The Radio Aerial"[6]

"The thing that he thinks is responsible for the trouble that has occurred since he has been married is red. Wherever he went he could see red. At a dry cleaning place, however, he had a yellow slip handed to him. He went out and wandered around and finally got to Sixth street where a nigger handed him a match and the nigger said: 'Santa comes but once a year.' All has a mystic meaning and is connected in some way with his trouble. He has not yet, formulated the exact process by which it works."[7]

" . . . THE FAMOUS DR. CROOKSHANK THINKS THE WHITE RACE SPRANG FROM THE CHIMPANZEE, THE BLACKS FROM GORILLAS, AND YELLOW PEOPLE FROM THE ORANG-OUTANG / An Orang-outang With Almond Eyes . . . Like The Chinese Child / . . . A Chimpanzee . . . [With] The . . . Intelligent Eyes . . . Of White Men / Africans . . . Squat On Their Haunches . . . Just Like Gorillas . . . And Live In Tree Tops . . . Like The Great Apes"[8]

187

NOV-14-1921
CAUFIELD & SHOOK
PHOTO.

192

"SCIENCE FINDS A TERRIFIC HEAT RAY THAT MELTS DIAMONDS AND BATTLESHIPS / . . . A Californian Has Harnessed Sun Beams And Turned Them Into The Greatest Known Force / . . . His New Ray . . . Focused Upon A Battleship, Will Melt It To The Waters' Edge"[9]

"For years he has had the gift of prophecy and is able to foretell events with accuracy . . . He has been with Jesus on earth and washed the blood from his back. Has heard voices for years. There was at one time a great conflict between two spirits—a good one and a bad one, each struggling for the mastery. Finally this conflict has quieted down. Thinks he foretold that he was going to dislocate his arm. Has done many good things such as killing and cutting the throats of sexual perverts, has murdered a good many of them and thinks he has done a good job. Now is in a cloud and cannot see the light."[10]

"SURGERY'S DARING NEW EXPERIMENT TO TEACH US PERFECT LOVE / Spleen Removal Science's Latest Thrust Against Human Cruelty And Revenge Aimed To Turn Demons Into Angels / . . . The Spleen Can Poison The Blood . . . The Heart And Then The Brain / Ann Bobar, Pretty New York Flapper . . . Slew Her Brother With A Breadknife . . . In A Frenzy Of Splenic Rage"[11]

"OUTLAW BLOOD MADE THIS CHOIR-GIRL A DEMON / Alienists See In Her Self-Confessed Slaying Of Two Relatives A 'Throwback' to Weird Indian Tribal Vengeance / Pretty Mrs. Tillie B. . . . In Jail On The Charge Of Murdering Her Father-In-Law And His Wife"[12]

"Has been living in the public for three years; is Queen of the Rockies; everybody sees her all of the time . . . She belongs to the soldiers; they told her she must not work anymore. Then she struck oil in Wyoming and became a millionaire. The American Soldiers, her men, (she has fifty-six husbands) are looking after it for her. She fell heir to the Almighty God's power, although she cannot use this herself but they are using it for her. This power of Almighty God is a machine . . . It is all in the Scripture that she is going to be the American Queen. She gets communications through a machine which talks to her and about her. Everybody around her talks about her all day long. She does not like to talk about this matter because it is too sacred."[13]

"SCIENCE FINDS NEW ANIMAL THAT 'LIVES' WHILE DEAD / Astonishing Secret, Just Discovered, Of The Tiny Bear Animalcule's Rigid Trances, Which May Solve Problems Of The 'Divine Spark' Within Us"[14]

"He says that on May sixteenth of the present year he went to a drug store at the corner of Broadway and Baxter Avenue in Louisville and told the clerk there that this was 'Resurrection Day' and that he was trying to get into Cave Hill Cemetery to dig up his wife. Something inspired him, he said, that he was going to see her and this inspiration came while at Keith's Theatre. He says he was going to resuscitate her by removing the embalming fluid and injecting hog's blood into her veins and connecting her veins with his and in this way keep her alive.

"He is going to build another story to his house and install therein a moving picture gallery, tennis court, bowling alley, swimming pool and make it a place of recreation. Says that he is the smartest man on earth and also one of the strongest and that to knock him down would require that he be struck with a hammer. Also speaks of going into the construction business when he leaves here, building railways and bungalows. Is also going to start a taxicab service of five taxis, each carrying twenty people, which will run between New Albany and Jeffersonville and Anchorage, and the fare will be only five cents."[15]

"WHAT ARTIFICIAL HABITS DO TO CITY FOLKS / Scientific Warfare Now Raging Over 'Straphanger's Slouch,' 'Cinderella Feet,' And Other Curious Physical Conditions Caused By Metropolitan Life / . . . Shoe Measurements Vary From City To City . . . New York and Chicago Average 4½"; Largest, Philadelphia And Pittsburgh, Average 5½" "[16]

———————

"EXPLODING THE ROMANCE OF ROYALTY'S DARLING / How The Adored American Soubrette Sneered At Europe's Nobility And Millionaires To Marry A Newark Piano Mover, And Now—The Wretched Result"[17]

"She heard tapping and voices in the house telling her to get out. She also saw radium pictures on the wall. Ran out of the house told her sister not to come in. She went back into the house and it was awful. She believes in mind reading, 'I have been having these communications for two weeks.' Her hearing is very keen. One morning about three o'clock she heard groaning, shrill shrieking and babies crying. She went out on the back porch and a voice told her to stay in the house or she would get killed, then the key was turned on her. She heard tappings all over the house . . . has heard . . . messages . . . got them continually can tell all sorts of things. Sometimes gave her silly messages. She gets them from all angles, some are friendly and some are not. This is accomplished by certain instruments—wall things. In City Hospital X-Ray is operating all the time. There were shrapnel pits and pumps. In May a year ago at home sometimes she could not sleep at night. Something was crushing and pulling her. Something was trying to hurt her—continually something is trying to hurt her here and again there, all over her body.

"The X-Ray is pumping her all the time. Sometimes it seems as though the bed is very much heated—she often gets up in the night and examines the bed but can see nothing. Saw in the Highlands queer machinery floating through the air. Telescopes have also been used on her. She is stolen property landed here. The radio pictures she saw on the wall were ugly faces."[18]

———————

195

196

"SCIENCE PROCLAIMS MAN A MERE MECHANICAL

ENGINE / Startling New Theory Scores The Soul And Declares A Drop Of Water And A Spark Created Human Life, Challenging Both The Scriptures And Darwin"[19]

" 'I knew years ago that I was crazy. The only way I know that is because we do not know how we were born or how we got into this world . . . Why do girls have their hair cut short? I'am going to live to be an old man and I want my wife to have long hair. How can a man stand before a woman or how can she expect him to stand before her when she hardly has any clothes or hair. What is the Government coming to when it allows itself to get into that kind of shape.' "[20]

"STARTLING SECRETS READ BY SCIENCE IN A SINGLE HAIR / . . . A Cross Section Of A Blonde Girl's Hair [Has] Concentric Rings Like Those Of A Tree Trunk / A Cross Section Of An Athlete's Hair [Has] A Strong Pigment Tube . . . / A Hair From A Strong Man's Head [Has] An Unbroken Central Circle Of . . . Filament Indicating Physical Strength"[21]

———————————

"SCIENCE PREDICTS THE FIRST 'LABORATORY MAN' BY 1951 / He Will Be Incubator Born In An Age of Synthetic Steaks, Sun Power, And Purple Oceans, Says Professor Haldane"[22]

" 'Aint't got no father, aint't got no mother, never had any father or mother. Was born from milk cows. Martie always treated me mean, had me handcuffed all of the time. I always call myself twenty-eight years old. I have plenty of money, millions of dollars, pretty near all of the automobiles in this country are mine, I made them for everybody. I have plenty of gold. All of the gold is mine. This is a place I built a long time ago, the place where they kill everyone.' "[23]

" . . . 'In a way, I am married to the State of Kentucky. I was just recently married, married to Jesus . . . I am intentioning bornation. Also discovered America, that is what they call a glide away.' He says he just put me here to sign claims."[24]

" 'I know the law. I am the head of it.' He says he is a student of degenrates . . . 'I was afflicted at birth, was helpless. The Government raised me from the cradle up.' Raised him just to make a fool out of people. 'This has been going on all my life . . . I am a natural born degenrate by birth.' . . . He says he was not in the Army but was recognized. He communicates by aerial, radio, etc. This began in his home—the University of Louisville came in and did it at home and the same thing exists now. When young he marched under English colors and later marched under United States colors. 'Of course England takes care of degenerates.' "[25]

———————————

"The girl who sees and hears with her fingers/ . . .

The Mysterious Sixth Sense of Colleta Higgins Who 'Listens' To Music Without Hearing Sound And Recognizes Color By 'Touch' "[26]

" 'My uncle was an elocutionist. Someone has a mocking voice. Things that are troubling me are that there are only two holy pictures on the wall. I am proud and neat and want that fountain pen back. I am what I am. I honor that flag. My tears are honored. I am no girl to brag on myself. I am a girl that works. I have the honor blash. Popocatapell. My hair has been cut to dishonor me.' She gazed at the wall in a listening manner and said, 'They shall crush the serpent . . . When I get out of here I am going to spend money for missionary work' . . . She began to cry and said, 'I want those beautiful curtains that hung over my eyes at night taken away and burnt.' "[27]

"She says she has a gold womb, a gold heart, and a gold head. She has more than a million dollars in the State Bank. Claims ownership of one hundred and fifty automobiles, a store in Texas worth a million dollars and millions and millions of dollars in a bank at Springfield."[28]

"THE COUNTESS CHOSE DEATH RATHER THAN SHOW HER MOLE / . . . Her Executioners Were Commoners And The Identifying Birthmark Was On Her Hip, But Luckily, She Fainted And Then—With A Lightning Like Gesture, He Tore Away The Silk Which Surrounded The Countess' Side / There, As He Suspected, Was The Tell Tale Mole"[29]

"A LITTLE BRAIN CELL THAT TURNS BRUNETTES INTO BLONDES / Fascinating Experiments Now Being Conducted By A Woman Scientist Which May Change Complexions And Even Racial Colors At Will . . ."[30]

"She worked at the telephone office for about three years and while there, there were so many people shouting in her ears she thinks it dislocated her brain. A man shouted and she felt as though it was chiseling into her brain. She never worked at anything after that and it seemed as though she could not bear to have anyone speak to her in any tone of voice but a soft one . . . All her life she has pictured in her own mind what she liked to do, for instance getting married—she pictured the fellow in her own mind. She knows who he is but he is so much higher and superior to her she was afraid the family would kill her after she married him. This picture was so satisfying to her that she became very happy. Thinks she may have felt even a spirit of ectasy."[31]

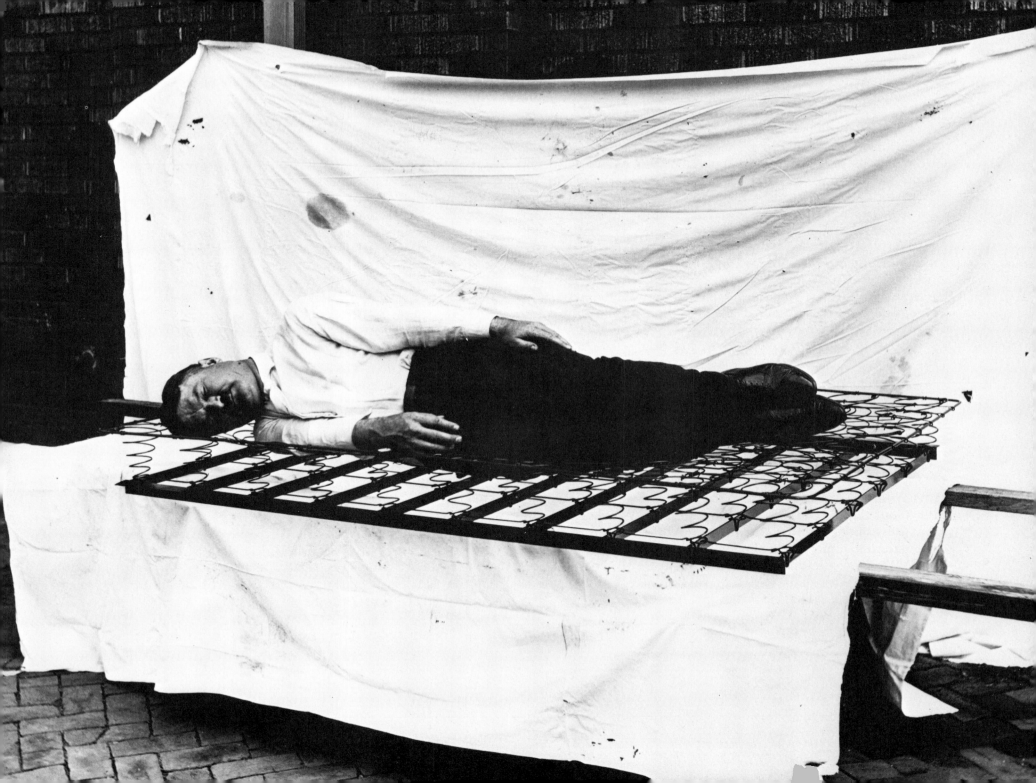

"His wife was operated on and had two tumors and appendix taken out. Got a shotgun, went across the street and fired it several times. . . . Began to tear up the walks, took off the coping of the porch, took the mortar from between the bricks, said he would get more work to do by doing that. Tore a large hole in the basement floor, his idea was to put some kindling wood in there. Would bury all the knives, forks, skillets and handsome carving set that was a wedding present, has never been located . . . Would be calm through it all and would never be angry at anyone, no matter what they said to him. Had a bone felon about eighteen years ago, a bone came out of his finger and left a hole there. Came running to his wife one day saying he knew what the cause of all their troubles, it was the finger that had the bone felon on it, and he intended to cut it off, then their luck would come back. Got the axe to cut it off, but his wife prevented his doing so. He was taken to court about his finger and was committed."[32]

"SURGERY'S AMAZING EXPERIMENT WITH LITTLE MARJORIE'S BIG TOE / The Doctors Spliced Live Wires To Dead Nerves, Turned A Switch — Presto! Her Paralyzed Foot Awoke"[33]

"Worked at L&N Shops — farmed — was in the Army for three years . . . Was somewhat disappointed when working at the shops that he did not get promotion . . . Worried some in the Army about the loss of time there which would make his promotion to a machinist slower. He thought his soul was lost and talked of suicide and left a request to his people as to where to bury his hand which he said he had been using as a preliminary to a sexual act with a girl."[34]

———

"STRANGEST BABY MYSTERY SINCE SOLOMON'S JUDGMENT / Two Men Claimed To Be His Father, Their Wives Disclaim Being His Mother / Was There Ever Such A Tangled Case Of 'Whose Baby Are You?' / Jolly Little, The Hero Of the Baby Mystery Which Has Amazed All Of New England"[35]

"At sixteen became involved with a girl — this girl had a child undoubtedly his own . . . At eighteen or twenty he was suddenly converted after praying a long time. It seemed to him as though rivers rushed into his soul and he loved things as he never loved them before. Married at twenty and wife lived only a short time and about three years afterwards he married his present wife. Has two children, boy fifteen and girl thirteen. When last girl was born his mother was present — she took it up into her arms and gave it to him saying, 'this is the illegitimate child who died and is now in you.' Paid little attention to this but later after his mother had died he dreamed that she came and set on his bed having the same child in her arms and around the child's head was a halo or crown. From that moment he loved his children, father, mother, wife and all. Since then love actually sprung up in his heart."[36]

———

"DID THE CHURCH CHOIR TRILBY HYPNOTIZE HER SVENGALI? / Amazing Case Of The Girl With Mona Lisa Eyes Who Cast A Strange Spell Over The Unfrocked Priest After He Had Taught Her To Sing / 'As She Focused Those Wonderful Eyes On Me All Else Was Blotted Out' / . . . 'She Hypnotized Me And I In Turn Hypnotized Her' "[37]

"He is very much in love with a girl in Adler's — intended to marry her but found out she was married. Afterwards heard she had obtained a divorce on his account. Says that when he was in jail practically all the people who roomed in the same house she did were in jail too — thinks maybe she had them sent there to protect him, she loved him so. Thinks that possibly they all got into jail by resisting his arrest . . . He hears voices continually coming from a distance. They sometimes seem to come from the living and sometimes from the dead. Once he heard his brother say he had given his father a black eye but was not able to verify it when he saw his father. These voices sometimes give him bad wishes and worry him but at other times he does not allow them to worry him. One time when he was in his boarding house he had just gone to bed and was lying looking out the door and saw a red devil running up the steps. He got up and looked around but could see nothing. Thinks house was haunted, one time—he saw a skeleton looking around the corner. A black cat jumped at him—crows fell from the roof, and he has heard things flap against the side of the house. A woman committed suicide there and several families have rented the house but have not stayed long. Thinks these things are death signals. When a fellow sees and hears those things, 'he is about half dead, isn't he?' When walking on the street these voices say mean things to him . . . Sometimes they have referred to him having homosexual habits. These voices have also told him that this girl in Adler's was in the same fix."[38]

"IS THE TRUTH DETECTOR A LIAR? / . . . The First Actual Legal Test Seems Likely To Put the O. K. On That Mysterious, Fascinating, New Drug Scopolamin / . . . H. J. Greel, Accused Of Receiving Stolen Goods, Under The Influence of Scopolamin And Surrounded By Texas Physicians, Awaiting His Admission Or Denial Of The Charges"[39]

"Believes the serum treatment he had in the Army is the cause of his present condition. He is very nervous and insists the Government must keep him as they ruined his health. The patient thinks if the Government would X-Ray him he would become well instantly . . . He always hears voices, that is since returning from the Army. Would tell mother that couldn't hardly hear her for the other voices. He would talk often of war and curse officers of Army. Would hear commands for drill and then drill himself."[40]

"Has felt since he was twenty-one that the United States Government has in some way interfered with his activities and has put someone over him who he feels should not be over him. He feels that someone with whom he is connected should be over this man . . . He thinks the Government sent him here when they should not have done so. The Government has sent others here which they should not have done. Before coming here felt that they were pulling him one way and some one else the other way . . . Has had at times a sensation as though something was crawling on the back of his neck."[41]

"He insists that he was drawn into an investigation of the I.W.W. for the government and, during this time, he had encounters with their direct influence in Louisville . . . 'I ate a roll and coffee in Thompson's lunch room between nine and ten in the morning and by four o'clock in the afternoon I was deathly sick. I believe that someone connected with them put something in my coffee. Again in Indianapolis I was warned by my friends that the I.W.W. was still trailing me. There never appeared any physical experience but I felt groggy for a period of three or four months and cannot explain it otherwise than by their influence. Again in Chicago, while acting as Assistant Manager in Thompson's lunch room, I was aware of their evil influence. Personally, I don't believe they are very bad fellows, most of them are good citizens. I have been among them and associated with them quite a little but their policies are bad.' "[42]

"LAYING BARE THE BURIED KREMLIN TREASURES AND HORRORS / How The Bolshevists While Entombing The Body Of Lenin, Accidentally Stumbled On The Secret Vaults And Subterranean Torture Chamber Of Ivan The Terrible / They Found . . . A Glittering Hoard Of Jewels And Gold / Feverishly The Bolshevists Continued Their Exploration"[43]

———————————

" 'My fundamental trouble was my spine, the syphillis ate that up. I can't stand much, it ate my brain up too because I haven't much sense now. I used to be intelligent as anybody until I got syphillis. I am just as happy as can be, I have Jesus in me. I got religion where I did those miracles, (tries to think of the place but fails). I have cast out devils and healed the sick and preached to them the knowledge of how to get salvation and I know that many have been saved by me. I healed some since I have been here but they made me cut it out. As a rule, I whispered to them here. I didn't tell them much here as I figured it wouldn't be much use.' At times the Lord pours down upon him special rays. These rays are inclined to be red and they make him very happy but don't last long enough. He states that a sinner could not stand in God's presence but he is in his presence. He is glad his old mind is gone because he will now get the mind of Jesus. Old Jack Downing is perishing and Jesus is a little infant growing within him."[44]

"JOHN D'S SECRET OF NEW YOUTH AT 85—BUTTERMILK / Richest Man In The World Went Hungry For Years, Built Up His Health As He Did His Fortune And Can Now Eat Just Like Any Other 'Normal Person' "[45]

Notes

1. Louisville *Herald*, March 29, 1924.
2. *Herald, Sunday Feature*, January 27, 1924.
3. Central State Hospital of Kentucky, Clinical Records, Case #21136, 1926.
4. *Herald, Sunday Feature*, August 26, 1923.
5. State Hospital Case #21171, 1922.
6. *Herald, Sunday Feature*, December 7, 1924.
7. State Hospital Case #21794, 1928.
8. *Herald, Sunday Feature*, October 12, 1924.
9. *Herald, Sunday Feature*, June 15, 1924.
10. State Hospital Case #21144, 1926.
11. *Herald, Sunday Feature*, August 3, 1924.
12. *Herald, Sunday Feature*, December 28, 1924.
13. State Hospital Case #20657, 1925.
14. *Herald, Sunday Feature*, October 21, 1923.
15. State Hospital Case #19254, 1922.
16. *Herald, Sunday Feature*, September 23, 1923.
17. *Herald, Sunday Feature*, June 22, 1924.
18. State Hospital Case #20612, 1925.
19. *Herald, Sunday Feature*, September 2, 1923.
20. State Hospital Case #20016, 1923.
21. *Herald, Sunday Feature*, January 13, 1924.
22. *Herald, Sunday Feature*, November 9, 1924.
23. State Hospital Case #20292, 1924.
24. State Hospital Case #21230, 1927.
25. State Hospital Case #20553, 1925.
26. *Herald, Sunday Feature*, April 8, 1923.
27. State Hospital Case #19867, 1923.
28. State Hospital Case #19906, 1927.
29. *Herald, Sunday Feature*, August 3, 1925.
30. *Herald, Sunday Feature*, February 24, 1924.
31. State Hospital Case #21224, 1926.
32. State Hospital Case #20302, 1922.
33. *Herald, Sunday Feature*, October 26, 1924.
34. State Hospital Case #20921, 1926.
35. *Herald, Sunday Feature*, May 18, 1924.
36. State Hospital Case #20885, 1927.
37. *Herald, Sunday Feature*, January 7, 1924.
38. State Hospital Case #20473, 1925.
39. *Herald, Sunday Feature*, November 25, 1923.
40. State Hospital Case #19355, 1922.
41. State Hospital Case #20949, 1926.
42. State Hospital Case #19777, 1923.
43. *Herald, Sunday Feature*, July 20, 1924.
44. State Hospital Case #20539, 1925.
45. *Herald, Sunday Feature*, September 21, 1924.

209

THE GANG
THAT PUT
CLOWN
Cigarettes
OVER

211

Sunday Feature

Taken at Falls 1920

214

"I want you to go on to picture the enlightenment or ignorance of our human conditions somewhat as follows. Imagine an underground chamber, like a cave with an entrance open to daylight and running a long way underground. In this chamber are men who have been prisoners there since they were children, their legs and arms being so fastened that they cannot turn their heads. Behind them and above them a fire is burning, and between the fire and the prisoners runs a road. . . ."

—Plato, The Republic[1]

One hundred and fifty thousand people subscribed to the Sunday papers,[2] and probably a hundred thousand more read bits and pieces of them. The magazine feature sections of these papers printed stories about the predicaments of rich people and the newest discoveries of science. The stories were filled with names, places, prosaic details, and scholarly references; they were illustrated with photographs. But the photographs were cut into collages and the names and details did nothing but fill the empty spaces around the headlines. The stories were elaborations of news accounts that were themselves literary transformations and elaborations of actual events. By the time the stories were printed as Sunday magazine features, they had as much to do with real people or actual facts as *Pilgrim's Progress* or the *Odyssey*[3] had to do with actual journeys. The stories of the rich were made into moral tales, and the stories of science became miraculous accounts. The men and women who read them spent the morning of what was still a religious day deciphering parables as profoundly dangerous as those told in the poetry of lunatics.

During the month of February 1925, the newspapers changed the struggles of a man named Floyd Collins into one of those stories. It took them two weeks to tell it. Collins wasn't a rich man, even though he wanted to be; and he wasn't a scientist, even though he knew more than most. He had been trapped while exploring a cave in central Kentucky on January 30, and died in it sometime between February 12 and February 16. By the time the people who tried to rescue him had found his body, fifty reporters[4] from sixteen big city newspapers and film crews from six motion picture studios[5] had turned him into a popular martyr. On the first Sunday of the newspaper story, 20,000 people[6] from sixteen states[7] turned a country road into an eight-mile traffic jam[8] to get a look at the hole he was in. Hundreds of ordinary people sent telegrams of advice; rich women sent physicians; fortune tellers sent predictions; imposters made claims; and little boys became lost.

Collins was a man who wanted to own an amusement park, but got trapped in the Tunnel of Love. Business and Industry tried to save him; experts and miners tried to help. The truth was that few of the experts knew what to do, and many of the miners were out of work or on strike. The only men who ever got close to him were a newspaper reporter who'd never met him, a business partner who'd become his rival, a fireman who wanted to pull his leg off, and a miner who kissed him good-bye. The harder they pulled to save him, the more Mother Earth sucked him in. The bigger the hole they made in Her, the quicker and stronger She squeezed it closed. Most of the city papers said She killed him; others said his family and friends had murdered him for his money; there were some who said he'd never been there to begin with. They might just as easily have said that he was a small businessman trapped by his own ambition, or a man-child who'd died crawling back into his mother, or even a novice who'd failed an initiation during a winter solstice.[9] It is difficult and complicated to tell what happened, but even that is easier than to account for what the newspapers thought it meant and what their readers imagined.

Collins was trapped in Sand Cave, in Barren County, a few miles over the line from Mammoth Cave in Edmonson County. The limestone under the ground was pocked and rotten. There were caves everywhere; there were 3,000 sinkholes.[10] Woodland Indians had lived and buried their dead in the caves 1,000 years before Christ's body was shut away.[11] When the whites dug saltpeter from Mammoth Cave they found the body of a woman surrounded by whistles, pendants, beads, and feathers.[12] They said it was an Indian Mummy. In 1820, a scholar visited them and went away talking like a man who'd seen a ghost. "The entrance to the infernal abodes of ancient mythology is most forcibly called to mind. Here . . . Virgil might have found a hell formed to his mind . . . this [is a] tomb of nature. . . ."[13] A hundred years later, Mammoth Cave had become an income property that paid regular dividends like a shrine that had become a public utility. Billy Sunday, the Christian evangelist, said that the cave made him feel "like a small piece of nothing dropped in the infinite."[14] That feeling cost a dollar to get inside and four dollars to stay all day. The money went to two old ladies in San Francisco, who'd been left that piece of Mother Earth by a doctor, their uncle.[15] The number of people who visited the cave varied with the state of the world. Forty thousand—a record number—made the descent during one of the years of the First War.[16] There were cave exhibits at the Kentucky State Fair for those who couldn't travel. The one in 1923 featured fish with no eyes and "the mummy of a monkey . . . which antedates by one million years . . . the famed King Tut."[17]

The biggest business in the area was the cave, but there were others. There was Great Onyx Cave, Colossal Cavern, Great Crystal Cave, Dorsey Cave, Salt Cave, Indian Cave, Parlor Cave, Diamond Cave, and Doyle's Cave of the One Hundred Domes.[18] They were all owned and operated by men who would have charged admission to the Apocalypse or the Crea-tion, depending on which came first. At the center of it all was Cave City, which served the tourists the way Lourdes served pilgrims. The only difference was that the men who ran the Cave City hotels tried to make their own miracles. In 1915, a Louisville man named G. D. Morrison formed the Mammoth Cave Development Company with the help of a vice president of the Fidelity-Columbia Trust Company and the owner of a Louisville men's store.[19] They hired a sewer engineer to sneak into Mammoth Cave and make a few surveys.[20] In 1921, Morrison convinced the Louisville & Nashville Railroad to lease the Development Company 100 acres of land three and a half miles from Mammoth Cave.[21] Somewhere underneath those 100 acres were the passages the sewer engineer had surveyed. Morrison's workmen drilled for a year, telling anyone who asked that they were looking for onyx.[22] Once they broke in, Morrison strung some electric lights inside, built a hotel, and opened for business. He'd made himself a back door. He called it the New Entrance to Mammoth Cave. He also called it "a miniature Atlantic City in the heart of Kentucky."[23] He said he had plans to build a $20,000 elevator in his hotel lobby, so that his guests could comfortably descend to the caverns below.[24] There were other people with other plans. A group of Chicago investors, headed by a member of the Glen Oaks Country Club, announced that they had purchased 300 acres of land three miles north of the cave.[25] They planned to construct a private eighteen-hole golf course, to be called the Blue Grass Country Club. They intended to solicit membership of Midwestern businessmen who couldn't be bothered to travel all the way to Florida for a vacation. Whoever had sold them the land hadn't told them that it was so leached by ground water that one of their greens was bound to turn into a sink-hole overnight.

While Morrison planned his underground elevator and the golfers sited their fairways, the local people were filing their own claims. Floyd Collins had more patience and less money than most of them. He was one of nine children, raised in a log cabin. His father, Lee, was a poor farmer who did a little trapping. Floyd, his brother Homer, and his brother Marshall, made a bare living cutting timber into railroad ties for the Louisville & Nashville and rafting them down the Green River.[26] In 1917, when he was twenty-seven, Floyd followed a groundhog that was caught in a trap down a hole on his father's farm.[27] The hole turned into a passage that led to a cavern.[28] He called it White Crystal Cave. He owned one-half and his father owned the other. They went into business. They sold options on the cave to a man named Johnny Gerald who'd made a little money buying and selling tobacco. He and Floyd took turns: one of them stood on the side of the road and tried to talk the tourists inside; the other guided them down Grand Canyon Avenue to see Nanny Ramsey's Flower Garden of gypsum crystals.[29] In 1921, while Floyd was standing on the road, he stopped a curator of anthropology from the Chicago Field Museum. The man hired him as an assistant. Floyd helped him for three years, and learned enough to know that he liked the caves better than the road.[30] He and Gerald began to argue about whose turn it was to be inside.[31] Business got tougher and tougher. One man turned his truck into a billboard and drove it up and down. His competitors put a stop to it by burning it. Another man picked a fight with Floyd and tried to run him off, but Floyd gave him a beating.[32] He and his father start-ed to argue about renewing Johnny Gerald's options when they expired on January 1, 1925. Lee wanted to renew them, but Floyd wanted to be free. Lee threatened to sue him, but Floyd wouldn't budge. So Lee renegotiated Gerald's option on his own half of the cave, but didn't tell Floyd a thing. He made the deal behind his own son's back.[33] By then, Floyd had begun to look middle-aged.[34]

In the middle of January 1925, Floyd signed a contract with a man named Doyle and another man named Ed Estes to explore a rock overhang called Sand Cave on Doyle's farm.[35] Doyle and Estes agreed to give Floyd half-rights to anything he found there.[36] There was a story that men who worked for Mammoth Cave had once dynamited the overhang.[37] The day before Floyd went down, he showed Estes a skull he'd found in a cave, and then gave it to Estes's son, Jewell. He said he was afraid of not coming out.[38]

On Friday, January 30, he went into the cave. He crawled down into the dark, on his belly, into a narrow passage. He slid fifteen feet straight down, then twisted through 100 feet of loops that sloped at thirty degrees. He dropped straight for eight feet, and then crawled for fifty feet more between loose rock walls until he reached a small cavern. He lay on his belly, looking down into a fifty-foot pit, twenty-five feet long and ten feet wide.[39] He went down into it looking for a passage, but it was closed. He scaled the walls and headed back the way he came. He kicked a rock that knocked some stones that started a slide that trapped him. He was caught 125 feet deep in the ground, in a space eight inches high and twelve feet long. The air was sixteen degrees. He was facing up in the direction he'd come, but there was a seven-ton boulder on his left foot. He lay in mud and black night, with water dripping on his head.[40] On Saturday morning, Estes sent Jewell into the tunnel. Floyd told him to go tell his brother Marshall and then come back and stay with him in the dark. Jewell grabbed some broken stalactites and crawled out.[41] Marshall came with his other brother Homer, and a crowd of men came with blow torches to heat the rock, and chisels and hammers to break it. They worked all day, but they couldn't free him.

On Sunday, Floyd was briefly reported on the front page of the *Courier*. On Monday, February 2, the *Herald* mistakenly reported that he'd been freed. By then, local and regional papers and the Associated Press had decided to change him into a story. They turned him into a headline because similar things had happened before. In 1922, Floyd and a photographer from the *Herald* had been trapped for two days in White Crystal Cave.[42] While Floyd dug a way out, the photographer had taken a picture of him that was circulated as a postcard and newspaper illustration in the state.[43] Other people had been trapped in other places before that. Sometime between 1920 and 1925, a minister had been falsely rumored and then mistakenly reported by Nashville papers to have been lost in a cave in northern Tennessee.[44] In December 1906, a miner who worked for the Edison Electric Company in Bakersfield, California, had been trapped in an overturned automobile when the roof of a communications tunnel had collapsed. His predicament and rescue on December 22 had been reported throughout the country.[45] When the Louisville papers first heard about Floyd, they recognized his name and remembered Mr. Morrison's subterranean elevator; the Chicago and Nashville papers who followed the lead of the *Courier* and the *Her-*

ald Post were already familiar with the reputation of Mammoth Cave; and the East Coast papers which subscribed to the Associated Press recognized the dramatic possibilities of a cave rescue. If Floyd had been saved as the *Herald* reported, the story would have ended; but Floyd remained trapped, and so his story spread and changed its nature. By Thursday, February 5, it had become a variety of moral tale known as a tragic disaster, in which the protagonists always suffered the consequences of their own immoderate appetites and ambitions.

On Monday, Homer Collins told a *Herald* reporter that he'd spent Sunday night in the tunnel with his brother. "Floyd told me that last night he dreamed of white angels riding in white chariots drawn by white horses . . . he saw chicken sandwiches [and] a red hot stove . . . I heard him praying . . . 'Oh Lord help me. I'm going home to the angels.' "[46] Homer offered $500 to any surgeon who could crawl into the passage and cut off his brother's leg.[47] People arrived from nearby counties and tried to crawl down the tunnel to be heroes. Hundreds of men stood around the hole telling one another what to do and offering each other a drink.[48] They'd ask Homer or Marshall for permission, and then crawl in carrying blankets and gloves, thermoses of coffee, bottles of milk, and cans of soup. Some of them went halfway down before they got frightened and stuffed the blankets and bottles and cans into the nearest crevice; they'd come out and tell everyone how grateful Floyd had been and exactly what he'd said.[49] The newspapers in Louisville and the telegraph office in Cave City began to get telegrams of advice. A doctor from Des Moines said he'd amputate Floyd's leg if they sent an airplane to get him; a man from Brooklyn suggested a screw jack;[50] a man from Schenectady suggested a flat iron hook; a man from Detroit suggested a welding torch; and another from Kansas City suggested a small electric drill.[51] The Louisville & Nashville dispatched a special train from Louisville to carry a pneumatic drill, a crew of stone masons from a monument company, a fire department lieutenant named Burdon, looking for a promotion, and a sweet-faced, nineteen-year-old reporter from the *Courier* named Skeets Miller. As soon as Burdon got off the train, he told a *Louisville Post* reporter that the only way to save Floyd was either to dig a shaft down behind him, or to crawl in and pull his leg off. He convinced Homer and Marshall to let him strap a harness to Floyd, connect it to a windlass, and pull him out like a worm from a hole. By the time he was ready, Homer and Marshall had passed out and been carried away.

Once Floyd's brothers were gone, his former business partner took over. Johnny Gerald told Burdon that if he tried anything, he'd kill him.[53] He chased away the stone masons. He wouldn't deal with any outsiders. At midnight, Monday, he crawled in, followed by a college president from Bowling Green and a former Army lieutenant who taught mathematics. They cleared rock from Floyd's body, freed his hands, widened the passage, and fed him coffee, milk, and grape juice. Floyd told Johnny that "he'd rather have him get him out than anyone else in the world."[54] The college president crawled out and announced that he was going to interrupt the Southern tour of his basketball team and order the boys to the rescue.[55] The stone masons from Louisville left the next morning. They said the rescue camp was a cross between a country fair and a

circus.[56] Five hundred men crowded around in front of the cave. People complained about pickpockets and tire thieves.[57] The president of the People's Bank of Cave City and the City Marshal asked the Governor to send a National Guard officer and a chief engineer to direct the rescue work.[58]

In the middle of the confusion, sometime on Tuesday, while Gerald was taking a nap and the college president was looking for his basketball team, the boy reporter from Louisville led a crew of men into the tunnel. Skeets knocked some rock away, gave Floyd a drink, and conducted an interview. It began: "Death holds no terror for Floyd Collins, he told me . . . as I placed a bottle of milk to his lips. . . ." Then it ran: "I have been in the cave three times . . . I am very small . . . I am confident . . . I lead the way . . . I have succeeded . . . It is terrible . . . I went first. . . ."[59] His paper headlined "COURIER JOURNAL MAN LEADS 3 RESCUE ATTEMPTS."[60] That night, he pulled a shining electric bulb with him into the tunnel and left it looped around Floyd's neck to keep him warm. The next day, the *Courier* printed a front page picture of Lee Collins shaking his hand. Lee was a bent old man who'd taken his hat off. Skeets stood young and tall as a prince. " 'Skeets The First' Is Cave City Ruler/Modest Young Miller Is Hero Of Town With Unwavering Determination."[61] He had crawled into the deep pit and returned to tell the world. People followed him everywhere. In spite of danger and fame, he still acted like a boy: "I wish you'd . . . tell my mother that there isn't any real danger because I know she'll be worried."[62]

The more people admired Skeets, the more Johnny Gerald resented him.[63] Johnny chased him away on Wednesday morning and led ten men into the hole. He chipped at the boulder that held Floyd's foot until Floyd told him he was free. The crew headed back to get a piece of canvas to drag him out. They were fifty feet from him when the tunnel collapsed.[64] Five days of digging had loosened the roof and weakened the walls. The heat of the work had thawed the frozen mud that had helped hold the rock in place.[65] Gerald broke through again twelve hours later. Floyd's foot was still caught. It had never been freed. He'd been delirious. He was dying of pneumonia. A young miner from Central City named Maddox gave him the last food he ever ate. He mumbled and whispered, "Maddox, get me out . . . why don't you take me out . . . kiss me good-bye, I'm going.[67] Maddox saw purple circles around his eyes and two front teeth made of gold. He kissed him good-bye.[68]

The experts came to save Floyd the next day. Kentucky Governor Fields ordered two detachments of soldiers under the command of Adjutant General Denhart to bring order to Cave City; he asked T. J. Carmichael, a superintendent of Kentucky Rock Asphalt and a member of the state Geological Survey, to direct rescue operations; and he requested W. D. Funkhouser, a University of Kentucky professor of anthropology and zoology, who had conducted archeological surveys of the area, to offer his advice.[69] The Louisville Gas and Electric Company sent a geologist who had made surveys of the area for them;[70] and Mrs. Emma Blaine, formerly Miss Znita McCormick of McCormick International Harvester of Chicago, dispatched Dr. William Hazlitt, a prominent surgeon, to cut off Floyd's leg.[71] Newspapers from New York, Chicago, St. Louis, Kansas City, Memphis, Nashville, Knoxville, Indianapolis, Atlanta, New Orleans, and Dallas sent their reporters.[72] The Red Cross set up a complete field hospital on one of the slopes overlooking the camp, and the soldiers strung barbed wire in a perimeter fifty yards beyond the bluffs that surrounded the rock overhang.[73] Outside the wire, vendors sold hot dogs, sandwiches, and coffee to tourists who had begun to arrive from Michigan, Illinois, Indiana, and Tennessee, and from Georgia, Alabama, Florida, South Carolina, and Louisiana.[74] Inside the wire, the experts agreed that the tunnel had become too dangerous, and that the safest way to rescue Floyd was to dig a shaft until it reached the boulder that pinned him.[75] None of them believed that they'd find him alive,[76] and most of them thought he was dead already.[77] The newspapers explained it this way: Homer and Marshall had passed out; Lee was an old wreck; Johnny Gerald had threatened a fireman and chased away a young hero. The only things Floyd's friends and relatives had managed to do was start arguments with nice people and bring the roof down on their own heads. They were amateurs who had made fatal mistakes. The experts would solve everything. The same military discipline and professional organization that had won the First War would prove its worth by saving a corpse.[78]

Carmichael of Kentucky Rock Asphalt Company organized 300 volunteers into three shifts. Some of them worked for the same company he did; others worked for the Louisville & Nashville Railroad,[79] some were out-of-work miners from the eastern Kentucky coal fields, and others were striking miners from Muhlenberg County in the western fields.[80] The miners said that Floyd would be squeezed to death before they got near him. The Squeeze, they said, always happened when the walls of a mine tunnel became weak, and hydraulic pressure pushed the floor up to the ceiling.[81] They estimated that the tunnel was closing at the rate of one-fourth inch an hour.[82] In Boston, two Harvard geologists denied that such a thing could ever happen in a limestone region.[83]

The experts at the cave began to monitor Floyd's condition electrically. They connected a "radio detector"[84] to the light bulb around his neck. They heard a grating noise every twenty seconds. Dr. Hazlitt, the surgeon from Chicago, said it meant that Floyd was gasping for breath.[85] A radio station in Chicago strapped a glowing bulb to the chest of a volunteer and then connected it to "a two stage audio amplifier and a one stage 'push-pull' amplifier." No one could hear a thing.[86] The engineers hauled two $10,000 steam shovels down the bluffs to the cave, but Dr. Hazlitt discovered that engine exhaust fumes were being drawn into the tunnel.[87] Johnny Gerald made a rude remark about the experts' shaft, and the Army threw him out.[88] Mr. Carmichael said it might cost $100,000 to dig Floyd up.[89] Three thousand people stood outside the wire and watched. They were too far away to see anything.[90]

The reporters began to look for news. They noticed that Floyd's faithful dog Shep hadn't eaten or slept for eight days. They learned that Floyd had once gone all the way to Louisville to buy his sweetheart, Alma Clark, a box of chocolate-covered cherries.[91] They listened to rumors. Neighbors hinted that Floyd had done it all for publicity, or had never been there in the first place, or had crawled out a secret tunnel. Marshall Collins, Fire Lieutenant Burdon, and Ed Estes said that Floyd had been murdered. They said Johnny Gerald had made a secret deal with Floyd's father to kill him and take over

Crystal Cave.[92] The A. P. correspondent from the *Chicago Tribune* asked Adjutant General Denhart what he knew. Denhart said he'd never heard any respectable citizen say anything about a hoax. The A. P. man said he'd heard that "the whole thing was an advertising scheme for the cave country and that the L & N and other powerful interests were behind" it.[93] He said he personally believed that Floyd was trapped but "he did not believe 'fake journalism' was dead."[94] Whether it was dead or not, the A. P. man wasn't the only one to have heard the rumors. Another A. P. man from Louisville had heard them,[95] and a doctor from Horse Cave had heard them too.[96] When the correspondent for the *Nashville Tennessean* went home for a day, he said fifty people had asked him if the whole thing wasn't a fake like the story of the minister lost in the cave.[97] On Saturday, February 7, all the correspondents from Louisville except Skeets met with correspondents from Cincinnati, Chicago, and Nashville in the Dixie Hotel in Cave City. They agreed that "jealousy, commercial strife, and personal enmity were far greater factors in the imprisonment of Floyd Collins than the forces of nature."[98] They waited until Monday to publish their new version of events. That gave the Adjutant General time to convince the Governor to convene a court of inquiry to stop the rumors[99] and it gave the newspapers' readers a Sunday free of too many ambiguities.

The Louisville Automobile Club issued directions on how to drive to Cave City.[100] Twenty thousand came for the show. They bought souvenirs and posed for tintypes in the meadow outside the barbed wire. Lee Collins moved through the crowd, introducing himself and handing out advertising for White Crystal Cave.[101] By noon, the only two restaurants in

Cave City had hung out "Bread and Water Only" signs. Louisville papers sold thousands of copies of their Sunday edition to people who couldn't get close enough to even see the barbed wire.[102] The General gave a Louisville minister permission to hold a service on one of the bluffs overlooking the hole. Five thousand people got down on their knees and prayed. They sang "Lead Kindly Light/Amid the encircling gloom/Lead Thou me on/The night is dark and/I am far from home/Lead Thou me on."[103]

On Monday, the Louisville *Herald Post*, the *Chicago Tribune*, the *Cincinnati Post*, and the *Nashville Tennessean* published copyrighted stories about the murder of a man who wasn't there. The newspapers described a paradox, but the Governor of Kentucky preferred the Truth. He ordered Adjutant General Denhart to remove the *Chicago Tribune* A. P. correspondent from his camp, and to begin a military inquiry. He also asked the A.P. to retract its man's story.[104] The court convened the next day. "The khaki, [the] shining accoutrements, and [the] highly polished boots recalled the days of the war and lent an air of impressiveness to the session."[105] The court listened to Lieutenant Burdon accuse Johnny Gerald, and then heard the mathematics professor from Bowling Green defend him. It heard a building contractor from Louisville accuse Anthropology and Zoology Professor Funkhouser of not knowing what he was doing, and watched while the professor fainted from the strain.[106] It listened to a dairyman from Louisville describe the drunks who stood around the cave entrance, and it heard testimony that doctors had put stimulants in Floyd's coffee.[107] It heard Lee Collins and Homer Collins defend Johnny Gerald,[108] and it took the testimony of two reporters who'd never heard any rumors.[109] General Denhart himself told of his conversation with the A.P. man from Chicago, and Edward Estes described how he'd first learned of Floyd's predicament.[110] While all this went on, a man from Haddam, Kansas, revealed that he was Floyd Collins. "Please contradict statements that I am buried alive in Sand Cave. Tell mother I am all right. Am coming home."[111] He said he had an American flag tattoo on his right arm, and a scar on the left of his navel that Johnny Gerald had given him.[112] Two little boys in Pittsburgh played Floyd Collins and trapped themselves in a cave near a beer vault.[113] A lady from Chicago wrote to Mr. Carmichael at Sand Cave to tell him that she knew Floyd was alive because her coffee grounds had settled in the shape of a heart.[114] The experts continued their own investigations. They sprayed banana oil into the down draft of the cave, and then tried to smell it rising from crevices that might have led to the original passage.[115] They hung two darning needles to the depth of their rescue shaft, and then crawled as far as they could into the passage with a powerful electromagnet. They calculated the angle and direction in which the needles strayed from the perpendicular, and in this way verified the progress of their digging.[116] On Friday the Thirteenth, they discovered they'd been wrong. The shaft was deep enough, but too far to the side. The radio-amplified light bulb and the electric darning needles hadn't worked.[117] They sent a man named Ed Brenner, a miner from Cincinnati, into the passage to make a noise to give them a clue. While they listened to him, he heard "somebody in a groan . . . like you hear a man that's got hurt in a hospital . . ."[118] They uncovered Floyd the next day. Dr. Hazlitt said he'd been dead five days.[119] Brenner said his "face was sharp and pointed; he had jaws like a bulldog. A sharp nose, a high forehead. His eyes were sunk and his mouth was open. His hair was black. I took his head in my hands and . . . washed his face."[120] He'd died in agony.[121] The Adjutant General fainted when he heard the news.[122]

They left Floyd where he was. The people in Cave City figured there'd been 60,000 tourists. Mr. Carmichael said it had only cost $25,000.[123]

Each of the local papers which reported on Floyd had used his predicament as an occasion to tell moral tales. The *Louisville Post* told a story about "Collins . . . trapped in a . . . grave more horrible than the weirdest imaginings of master fictionalists. Nature is moving against . . . human beings . . . like a master chess player . . . It has been a desperate struggle for cheap fame . . . if Collins dies, a monument should be erected on the mossy wall of the cave . . . bearing the inscription: 'A brave man died here . . . a martyr to the lust for glory.' "[124] The *Courier* published an allegory in which Floyd was the protagonist of a "tragedy in several acts" written by "Fate, the master playwright," whose subject was "the struggle between man and . . . Nature, unexorable," and whose dramatic effect was heightened by "Ignorance . . . Jealousy . . . and Greed."[125] During the first week of Floyd's imprisonment, the papers jointly elaborated a story in which Floyd was the victim, Nature was the deadly antagonist, Johnny Gerald was a traitor, and the engineers and National Guard were heroes in a battle. However, during the second week, the *Herald Post* published a paradoxical story that could only be understood by an audience already critical of its own surroundings. The *Herald Post* was joined by three other papers in three other major cities of the region, but it was not joined by the *Courier*. The *Courier* refused to elaborate the new parable because the story denied the salvation offered by an archetypal young hero from the *Courier's* own staff.[126] The *Courier's* version of events resembled a pleasant fairy tale in which a worthy man was helped by a young prince who, in turn, was aided by wise men and warriors. The *Herald Post's* version sounded like a paranoid delusion.

The Adjutant General who fainted when he heard Floyd was dead blamed the story of the hoax on a Chicago A.P. man who wanted to sell papers more than tell the truth. The truth was that the people of the area had been exchanging gossip and spreading rumors long before either the General or the reporter had come near them. Sons accused fathers, neighbors blamed neighbors, and people heard rumors because they had defamed the natural order of their surroundings. They had given nicknames to the Earth's mysteries; they had stood on the side of the road and told Her secrets like anecdotes; they had smashed holes in Her maze and sold tickets; they had crawled through Her bunghole and called it their front door. While they did all that, they cheated and threatened, and they envied and beat one another. They went into business.

The people who bought the papers in Louisville, Nashville, Cincinnati, and Chicago believed the rumors and the accusations because they had heard of such things before in their own cities. Between 1923 and 1925, stories of fraudulent business deals and crimes of passionate betrayal filled the front pages of city newspapers. In Louisville, there were the erotic disasters of Dr. Lewis, a drug addict who had murdered his wife; of Cecil Wells,[127] a commodities broker who had tried to castrate his best friend; and of William Zinmeister, a soft drink stand owner who had shot his daughter. There were the stories of the bunko schemes of Madame Dinler, who stole Josephine Traub's savings, and of sick Mr. DeFough, who robbed generous Mr. Coravitous. Each year, there were stories of business frauds on a grand scale. The papers told of how the Home Telephone Company was bought by the Cumberland Telephone Company through the connivance of bankers, businessmen, and elected officials who had told the public nothing but a series of lies. The papers published in serial the routines of James Duffin and R. V. Board, who juggled oil stocks and a wagon company until they themselves slipped into the hands of James Brown, the master magician. There were constant stories of partners against partners, brothers against brothers, deaths at opportune moments, and marriages of convenience. The papers reported how Elmer Schmidt had signed an insurance-suicide pact with William Werdeman, whom he planned to murder. They reported how William Haldeman had sued his brother Bruce to sell their father's newspapers to Robert Bingham, and how Bingham had bought the papers with money inherited from a woman who had died nine months after he'd married her. They told how William Sackett had become a rich man, then a senator, and finally an ambassador by marrying Olive Speed. The people who had learned about all these things remembered them as they read about Floyd Collins, the small businessman who was trapped by his own greed, failed by his own partner, betrayed by his own father, and libeled by his own neighbors. They hoped that a young prince would save him, but understood when he proved as helpless as the soldiers, the businessmen, and the experts.

When Floyd's audience read about him, they thought about themselves. Four years later, the story became a prophecy.

Notes

1. Book 7, translated by H.D.P. Lee (Baltimore, Md.: Penguin Books, 1955).
2. Louisville *Courier-Journal*, February 5, 1925.
3. Joseph Campbell, *The Masks of God, Occidental Mythology* (New York: Viking, 1970), Ch. 4, pt. 3.
4. *Courier-Journal*, February 16, 1925.
5. *Louisville Post*, February 5, 1925.
6. *Courier-Journal*, February 9, 1925.
7. *Louisville Post*, February 5, 1925.
8. Louisville *Herald*, February 9, 1925.
9. Mircea Eliade, *Rites and Symbols of Initiation* (New York: Harper Torchbooks, 1958), p. 52.
10. *Courier-Journal*, February 12, 1925.
11. Douglas Schwartz, *Conceptions of Kentucky Pre-History* (Lexington, Ky.: University of Kentucky Press, 1967); Robert Silverberg, *Mound Builders of Ancient America* (Greenwich, Conn.: New York Graphic Society, 1968), p. 227; *Archeological Survey of Kentucky*, Vol. II (Lexington, Ky.: Department of Anthropology, University of Kentucky Press, 1932).
12. *Archeological Survey of Kentucky*, Vol. II.
13. John H. Farnham, *Transactions of the American Antiquarian Society*, Vol I (1820), pp. 355–61.
14. *Courier-Journal*, February 8, 1925.
15. Louisville *Herald Post*, March 9, 1924; Louisville *Times*, December 1, 1923.
16. *Herald*, July 23, 1923.
17. *Herald*, September 12, 1923.
18. *Courier-Journal*, February 12, 1925.
19. *Herald Post*, August 31, 1926.
20. *Ibid.*
21. *Times*, April 19, 1923; *Herald*, July 23, 1923.
22. *Herald*, May 2, 1922.
23. *Herald*, July 23, 1923.
24. *Ibid.*
25. *Times*, May 19, 1923.
26. *Herald*, February 10, 1925.
27. *Courier-Journal*, February 8, 1925.
28. *Herald*, February 5, 1925.
29. *Courier-Journal*, February 8, 1925; *Louisville Post*, February 9, 1925.
30. *Courier-Journal*, February 16, 1925.
31. Louisville *Evening Post*, February 9, 1925.
32. *Ibid.*
33. *Louisville Post*, February 9, 1925; *Evening Post*, February 9, 1925; *Courier-Journal*, February 10, 1925.
34. *Louisville Post*, February 10, 1925.
35. *Courier-Journal*, February 15, 1925.
36. *Courier-Journal*, February 15, 1925; *Louisville Post*, February 2, 1925.
37. *Herald*, February 8, 1925.
38. *Herald*, February 5, 1925.
39. *Courier-Journal*, February 9, 1925, February 5, 1925.
40. *Louisville Post*, February 2–3. 1925.
41. *Courier-Journal*, February 15, 1925.
42. *Herald*, February 1, 1925.
43. *Louisville Post*, February 9, 1925.
44. *Courier-Journal*, February 14, 1925.
45. *Herald*, February 8, 1925.
46. *Louisville Post*, February 3, 1925.
47. *Louisville Post*, February 2, 1925.
48. *Louisville Post*. February 3, 11, 12, 1925.
49. *Courier-Journal*, February 8, 1925.
50. *Louisville Post*, February 3, 1925.
51. *Louisville Post*, February 4, 1925.
52. *Evening Post*, February 11, 1925.
53. *Louisville Post*, February 9, 1925.
54. *Louisville Post*, February 10, 1925.
55. *Louisville Post*, February 3, 1925.
56. *Louisville Post*, and *Herald*, February 4, 1925.
57. *Herald*, February 7, 1925.
58. *Herald*, February 3, 1925.
59. *Courier-Journal*, February 4, 1925.
60. *Ibid.*
61. *Courier-Journal*, February 5, 1925.
62. *Ibid.*
63. *Louisville Post*, February 4, 11, 1925; *Courier-Journal*, February 14, 1925.
64. *Louisville Post*, February 4, 1925.
65. *Ibid.*
66. *Courier-Journal*, February 17, 1925.
67. *Courier-Journal*, February 16, 1925; *Louisville Post*, February 5, 1925.
68. *Courier-Journal* and *Louisville Post*, February 5, 1925.
69. *Louisville Post*, February 4, 1925.
70. *Louisville Post*, February 16, 1925; *Herald*, February 13, 1925.
71. *Louisville Post*, February 4, 1925.
72. *Louisville Post*, February 5, 1925.

73. *Louisville Post*, February 6, 8, 1925.

74. *Ibid.*

75. *Louisville Post*, February 5, 1925.

76. *Ibid.*

77. *Louisville Post*, February 6, 1925.

78. *Courier-Journal, Louisville Post,* and *Herald*, February 6, 1925.

79. *Louisville Post*, February 10, 1925.

80. *Courier-Journal*, February 8, 1925. The miners from the eastern fields had been forced out of work by a seasonal decrease in demand for coal in a nation that still used most of it to heat its homes, not light them, and by a chronic depression in the price per ton combined with an equally chronic shortage of railway rolling stock (*Herald*, March 21, 1923). The miners from Muhlenberg had gone on strike with 6,000 others in April 1924, when the mine owners had offered them a 1917 wage scale (*Herald*, April 15, 1924). The strike had remained peaceful until February 9, when strikers in Greenville had fired hundreds of shots into the homes of two mine bosses (*Louisville Post*, February 9, 1925). A day later, several squads of forty armed men attacked the Rogers mine in Bevier, which had resumed operations as an open shop (*Louisville Post*. February 10, 1925). The same governor who sent an adjutant general and troops to supervise Floyd's rescue sent other troops to break the mine war in Muhlenberg.

81. *Louisville Post*, February 5, 1925.

82. *Louisville Post*, February 6, 1925.

83. *Herald*, February 11, 1925.

84. *Louisville Post*, February 6, 1925.

85. *Herald*, February 10, 1925.

86. *Louisville Post*, February 11, 1925.

87. *Louisville Post*, February 7, 1925.

88. *Louisville Post*, February 6, 1925.

89. *Louisville Post*, February 7, 1925.

90. *Herald*, February 9, 1925.

91. *Louisville Post*, February 6, 1925.

92. *Louisville Post, Evening Post, Herald, Nashville Tennessean, Cincinnati Post,* and *Chicago Tribune*, February 9, 1925.

93. *Courier-Journal*, February 15, 1925. The Louisville & Nashville Railroad had done more than lease 100 acres of land to Mr. Morrison for his New Entrance in 1923. It had been spending money since 1880 to control the political economy of Kentucky. In 1899, it had tried to prevent the election of an anti-monopoly, populist Democrat named Goebel as governor. When the election ended in a draw that went to the state legislature for final decision, the L&N carried 1,000 armed men to Frankfort to help the representatives to make up their minds. Goebel won the contest, but he was killed by an assassin the next day. Some people thought the L&N had something to do with it (Murray Klein, *History of the Louisville and Nashville Railroad*, New York: Macmillan Co., 1972; C. Vann Woodward, *Origins of the New South*, Baton Rouge, La.: Louisiana State University Press, 1966).

94. *Courier-Journal*, February 15, 1925.

95. *Herald*, February 13, 1925.

96. *Herald*, February 11, 1925.

97. *Courier-Journal*, February 14, 1925.

98. *Louisville Post*, February 7, 1925.

99. *Courier-Journal*, February 15, 1925.

100. *Courier-Journal*, February 8, 1925.

101. *Louisville Post*, February 9, 1925.

102. *Herald*, February 9, 1925.

103. *Ibid.*

104. *Evening Post*, February 9, 1925.

105. *Evening Post*, February 10, 1925.

106. *Evening Post*, February 11, 1925.

107. *Ibid.*

108. *Courier-Journal*, February 12, 1925; *Louisville Post*, February 13, 1925.

109. *Courier-Journal*, February 14, 1925.

110. *Ibid.*

111. *Courier-Journal*, February 12, 1925.

112. *Ibid.*

113. *Evening Post*, February 11, 1925.

114. *Courier-Journal*, February 16, 1925.

115. *Louisville Post*, February 9, 1925.

116. *Herald*, February 9, 1925.

117. *Herald*, February 13, 1925.

118. *Herald*, February 14, 1925.

119. *Louisville Post*, February 17, 1925.

120. *Herald*, February 18, 1925.

121. *Ibid.*

122. *Courier-Journal*, February 17, 1925.

123. *Herald*, February 18, 19, 1925.

124. *Louisville Post*, February 5, 1925.

125. *Courier-Journal*, February 8, 1925.

126. Carl Jung and C. Kerenyi, "The Psychology of the Child Archetype," *Essays on a Science of Mythology*, translated by R. F. C. Hull, Bollingen Series 22 (Princeton, N. J.: Princeton University Press, 1949).

127. *See* p. 53, note 43.

96682

FIRST SIX GRADES